"Grace C. Liu has written an impressive and inspiring book for younger and older readers alike. As the title, *Research to Empower,* suggests, the goal of research is not merely to accumulate knowledge, although that is clearly one important objective, but to empower researchers and society, in general, to make the world a better place. As Grace explains, empowering research topics are not confined to esoteric scientific questions. They include almost anything under the sun, ranging from such sociological issues as the role of mentorship in inspiring greater female participation in sports to finding the best way to bring affordable potable water to impoverished rural villages. This serious book, written in an engaging conversational style with occasional humorous asides, is for anyone who wants to understand the world in order to change it."

–*Dr. Alfred Watkins,* Founder and CEO,
Global Solutions Summit

"I have always said that we cannot win a football match by leaving 50 percent of the team on the bench! Women also contribute by bringing on board their hard work, intuition, solidarity, and perspective. Grace C. Liu belongs to this category of women who wants 'to inspire, support, and empower the next generation of aspiring young researchers in a vibrant way.' She shows generosity of spirit and wants to empower others. A great sentiment indeed. I would recommend this book to those who are keen to learn and are on a journey of discovery. The book is well written and in a style which makes it highly readable."

–*Dr. Ameenah Gurib-Fakim,* President of the Republic of
Mauritius (2015–2018) and Biodiversity Scientist

"*Research to Empower* is an extraordinary book that equips the next generation with essential tools to unlock the world of knowledge. Through its engaging and accessible approach, this guide offers invaluable guidance on conducting thorough research, critical thinking, and presenting findings effectively. It encourages curiosity, inspires creativity, and instills a passion for learning. It is an absolute must-read for anyone ready to make a positive change in the world."

    –Ms. Amy Meuers, CEO of National Youth
    Leadership Council, USA

"Grace C. Liu has written an extraordinary book that manages to show young people (like herself) how the often dreaded 'research project' can actually be simultaneously fun, interesting, educational, and even rewarding. Her friendly, practical writing style and the inclusion of plenty of appealing examples, illustrations, practical tips, and other elements make for an engaging and useful read. Grace also pays special attention to making the book accessible and useful to students who may not typically think of themselves, or be thought of by others, as having the skills and interest to do meaningful and impactful research. I would strongly recommend this book for use by students, teachers, parents, or others who want to support young people in their learning adventures. Having taught research and writing at the college and graduate levels, I can say without hesitation that I wish all of my students had read this book while they were in high school or junior high and if they hadn't done so by then, they could still benefit from it in college or in career and technical school. This is a much-needed book for which there are few, if any others, that are as enjoyable, well-written, and practical."

    –Dr. Brian Baird, Chair and Founder at National
    Museum and Center for Service, USA

"With her lively and engaging style, Grace C. Liu shows how doing one's own research is the key to critical thinking, real knowledge, and understanding as well as acquiring practical skills for achieving career goals and human fulfillment. This wonderful, insightful, and inspiring book is a joy to read. It will captivate inquisitive students from grade school to high school as well as serve as a guide for teachers and parents to be better at motivating students for a lifetime of inquiry-based learning. As Grace states, we cannot rely on tools like ChatGPT to replace our precious intuition, creativity, innovation, and independent thinking."

–*Dr. E. William Colglazier,* American Physicist,
the fourth Science and Technology Adviser
to the US Secretary of State

"Grace C. Liu's unwavering dedication to fostering curiosity and embracing intellectual exploration is truly inspiring. Through her words, she encourages young minds to unlock their innate inquisitiveness and seize the opportunities that research presents. Grace has artfully crafted a guidebook that will empower young students to navigate the realm of research with confidence and enthusiasm."

–*Dr. Giovanni Durante,* Principal of
Syosset High School, New York, USA

"The world of science is rapidly evolving and transforming in ways that make research and critical thinking more important than ever. Grace C. Liu eloquently and successfully breaks down concepts surrounding the process of scientific research, using engaging narratives and simple language to motivate younger minds toward research, investigation, and the pursuit of knowledge. I admire this effort by Grace to nurture 'thinking and curious minds' to fuel research in the modern world. I wholly recommend *Research to Empower* to anyone hoping to inspire the intellect of young people from all backgrounds."

–*Dr. Huadong Guo,* Director General of the
International Research Center of Big Data for
Sustainable Development Goals and Academician
of the Chinese Academy of Sciences

"In a world that needs science more than ever, Grace C. Liu brings inspiration and hope with a book that provides young people with the insight and the skills to explore and harness the transformative potential of research. She speaks with passion and the insight of personal experience to future change makers, and in ways that educators can and must take note of."

–*Dr. Heide Hackmann,* Director of Future Africa,
University of Pretoria, South Africa and Inaugural
CEO of the International Science Council

"Grace C. Liu's book, *Research to Empower* accomplishes a difficult task: writing about the elements of conducting research without sounding like a stale university lecturer! Her book, written primarily for a teenage audience, is filled with solid guidance on the hows and whys of various research methodologies, interspersed with personal anecdotes about her own experiences as a researcher, and a good dose of humor that her teen readers will appreciate. In her book's conclusion, Grace writes that she hopes her book 'inspires, supports and empowers' young researchers like herself. Without a doubt, she succeeds on all three counts."

–*Dr. James R. Delisle,* Professor of Education (retired),
Kent State University and Author of twenty-six
books including *The Gifted Teen Survival Guide*

"Against the backdrop of Grace C. Liu's own journey into the world of research, *Research to Empower* provides insightful tips and practical techniques for young researchers in an engaging, encouraging, and empowering way."
  –Dr. Jayshree Seth, 3M Chief Science Advocate
  and Corporate Scientist

"From an early age, we all have questions and curiosity about the natural world and society and want to understand the 'why' and 'how' of things. Recognizing the importance of cultivating these qualities, Grace C. Liu goes a step further and offers young students vivid guidance in her book *Research to Empower*. This book aims to nurture young researchers who can think critically and take action in the ever-changing world."
  –Dr. Michiharu Nakamura, President Emeritus,
  Japan Science and Technology Agency

"A sprinkle of fun and flavor to a seemingly daunting topic! Grace C. Liu's work is truly a precious jewel. While her choice of a humorous and spontaneous writing style makes this piece very enjoyable to read, she successfully manages to communicate her mature and insightful reflections on the essentials of the scientific process in a clear fashion. What's more, Grace generously shares real anecdotes of her personal experiences, to which aspiring researchers of all ages can relate—especially the young ones. At times when the connections between science and society have increasingly been difficult to bridge, Grace has certainly achieved her purpose of inspiring, supporting, and empowering new generations of researchers and conscious citizens."
  –Dr. Paulo Gadelha, President of FIOCRUZ
  (2009–2016) and Coordinator of the FIOCRUZ
  Strategy for the 2030 Agenda

"*Research to Empower: A Vibrant Guidebook for Young Students* by Grace C. Liu demystifies knowledge generation and makes the scientific process accessible to anyone interested in critical thinking and trying to make sense of our rapidly changing world. Grace writes with profound insight and wisdom on science in a captivating and accessible style that young and older readers can relate to. It takes great depth and understanding of science to be able to communicate this well with such a broad audience and to be able to do this as a teenager underscores how inspiring, generous, magnanimous, remarkable, and exemplary the author is not just identify and fill an important gap but to do it with humor and joy. The world needs more critical thinkers and innovators to address the multitude of complex challenges that face us. Grace's book lives up to its title by opening the door and providing the critical tools for young people to be inspired to leave the world a better place through science and innovation. A must-read for parents, students, and anyone who wants to understand science and the scientific method."

   –*Dr. Quarraisha Abdool Karim,* President of the
     World Academy of Sciences and Professor of
     Clinical Epidemiology, Columbia University

"While working with many outstanding students from around the world, I often encounter students who are interested in research but have no idea how to get started. I now have an answer. Grace C. Liu's *Research to Empower* offers a much-needed, engaging onramp to those students who would join knowledge-seekers like Grace that aspire to learn a little bit more about the world with each inquiry."

   –*Mr. Richard Rusczyk,* Founder and CEO of the
     Art of Problem Solving

"An impressive and inspiring writer herself, Grace C. Liu uses her passion and skill to encourage and, yes, empower others to embrace the critical value of research. Importantly, she understands and advocates for both research for purpose—whether to satisfy personal curiosity or transform the world—and the parallel need for communicating for impact. *Research to Empower* offers the keys to opening the doors of knowledge and opportunity for her generation to create the future."

    –Dr. Stuart Krusell, Senior Director, Global Programs,
       Sloan School of Management, Massachusetts
       Institute of Technology

"With advice both practical and entertaining, Grace C. Liu demystifies the process of starting research and illustrates, through her own grit and example, that research—even demanding, publishable research—is not out of reach for younger students who work hard and follow her step-by-step approach. Grace is as focused on the process of research—and the habits and skills it strengthens—as she is on the joys of the discoveries themselves. Accessible to younger readers, but not at all superficial, *Research to Empower* provides a compass to a whole new generation of intellectual explorers."

    –Dr. Tom Rogers, Syosset District Superintendent
       and CEO at Nassau BOCES, New York, USA

"False news, manipulation, depression, misogyny, these are realities each of us, particularly the young and therefore more vulnerable—or should I say less prepared—encounter far too often. But not if you are Grace C. Liu!

"With an open mind, eagerness to learn, and trust in science, Grace set her bright mind to work to research, analyze, and understand the reality around her, using the same tools that are so often used for negative purposes.

"She even goes a step further and shares the keys to her positive attitude and mindset with others. The result: a fun book, full of practical tips, hands-on advice, and illustrations. A playful book good to read for young and old(er)."

–*Dr. Veerle Vandeweerd,* Co-founder of the Global
Sustainable Technology and Innovation Conference
Series and Former Director (Environment and Energy)
of the United Nations Development Programme.

"Learning and researching are important life-long skills, especially in today's digital age when technology is making profound transformation of future of work and society. Based on her own research experience, Grace C. Liu's book provided the most vivid, inspiring, and practical guidance for young people who want to develop their research skills to empower them. Grace's own experience is also an excellent example for many young people who want to make the world better."

–*Dr. Xiaolan Fu,* Professor of Technology and
International Development and the Founding
Director of the Technology and Management
Centre for Development, University of Oxford

RESEARCH TO EMPOWER

A Vibrant Guidebook for Young Students

GRACE CHENXIN LIU

POST Hill PRESS

A POST HILL PRESS BOOK
ISBN: 979-8-88845-133-5
ISBN (eBook): 979-8-88845-134-2

Research to Empower:
A Vibrant Guidebook for Young Students
© 2024 by Grace Chenxin Liu
All Rights Reserved

Cover design by Conroy Accord

Post Hill Press
New York • Nashville
posthillpress.com

Published in the United States of America
1 2 3 4 5 6 7 8 9 10

To my family and research mentors.

Contents

Part One
Let The Games Begin!

Part Two
Game-In-Progress

Part Three
Level Up!

Author's Note

I present research like a game–and frequently use it as a metaphor–for you, the target audience, and to add a sprinkle of fun and flavor to a topic that seems daunting at first. Enjoy!

List of Boxes, Tables, Figures, and Photos

Boxes

Tables

Figures

Photos

Foreword

IT GIVES ME GREAT PLEASURE to endorse "Research to Empower", an extraordinary first book by Grace Liu. A teenager herself, Grace shares the ups and downs of her journey and her sources of inspiration that led to her discovery of research as a tool for inquiry and a source of empowerment.

Grace's success in publishing her research on the history of the barriers faced by women in fencing and her learning, during her research, of the processes that broke down the barriers to discrimination in women's fencing, has no doubt empowered her to write this book.

There is therefore a dual message in this book, a practical approach to undertaking research projects at school and the unexpected learning and the potential for other outcomes that can result.

The author has shared her approach to research in a practical manner that will no doubt appeal to many teenagers like herself who simply don't know where to begin a research project. It provides practical tools, exercises and examples. The author's examples of her success, reinforce her clear message that *"you can do it too"*.

Importantly, the book shows how individual research is more important than ever in a world where Artificial Intelligence (AI) has become prevalent everywhere, including in assisting students to write research papers. The book correctly points out that it is only through original research that one can learn to think critically, assess facts and determine whether there are true or false, derive independent conclusions and be innovative and creative.

The book also shows how independent research can be a wonderful journey, leading one down a path that perhaps no one has trodden on before and where the destination is, most excitingly, unknown. It is a journey that can lead to a hidden treasure, a discovery about oneself or the world. The author has made this discovery and has shared it with us all.

This book is therefore truly empowering for all young people. I hope that many teenagers, especially young girls will read this book with avid interest. It is intelligent, fun and well-written. Like the author, I hope that young readers realize that their research could result in far-reaching consequences that could result in them becoming tomorrow's leaders, changing the world and making it a better place for us all.

June 10, 2023
Dr. Marlene Kanga
President, World Federation of
Engineering Organizations, 2017–2019
National President, Engineers Australia, 2013
Vice President, International Network for
Women Engineers and Scientists, 2011–2017
Foundation Fellow, International Science Council

Research to Empower

*"Nothing has such power to broaden the mind as
the ability to investigate systematically and truly all
that comes under thy observation in life."*

–MARCUS AURELIUS (121–180 AD),
Roman emperor

MY STORY STARTED FROM HERE...

Growing up in suburban New York, I have been surrounded by people of color from first-generation and newly immigrated families. It's a continuous reminder of what it means to appreciate education changing people's lives.

Four years ago during sixth grade, I started researching the role of fencing in women's empowerment throughout history since I was an avid fencer myself. During this journey, I confronted a lot of challenges such as looking for a mentor, choosing research questions/topics, learning the methodology, staying motivated while having to spend time on schoolwork, and handling everything while having a life, for goodness' sake!

After many hurdles (I'll get to this part later—it's a whole chapter on its own), I never expected to end up presenting my research at multiple global conferences with professors and experts worldwide and finally publishing it in the *Journal of International Women's Studies*, a peer-reviewed journal and place where my work was verified by professional researchers in the field! The positive feedback from professors and experts was like energy drinks, fueling me and allowing me to realize the power of sharing knowledge with others. This felt empowering for me, the knowledge-sharer, too! Nothing felt better than the uncontrollable smile spreading across my face when I saw my name next to a completed, published journal paper that was already gaining downloads (from people outside of my family too)!

My efforts also opened the door for invitations to research opportunities with the United Nations (UN), publications in books, and opportunities to be an invited speaker on TEDx and the UN Sustainable Development Goals (SDG) Learncast podcast where I advocated for more support for teen researchers and advocates. My favorite and most vivid memories are from sharing my research experience, giving speeches, attending conferences, and, most of all, seeing young faces like mine light up with delight after receiving inspirational ideas.

I feel fortunate because I received so much help and overcame many difficulties. I know research isn't glamorous and many students are wandering their way through "the land of research," occasionally stumbling here and there or straying from the right path.

THE TURNING POINT...

One day, I was having lunch with my friend, who is from a recently immigrated, first-generation family with parents that barely speak English. She raved about spending sleepless nights scrutinizing and digging through website after website, organization after organization, and program after program—all just to look for a research mentor. When she mentioned the part about many research programs for high schoolers charging ridiculous amounts—around $3,000 to $20,000 just for supervising students to learn how to research—I choked on my sandwich! How could this happen?

I knew about the insufficient support for young researchers and how the existing resources are unevenly distributed. I have been in situations where I was the only young Asian girl in a research team, which is why I have strived to fight against the lack of inclusiveness in education in these past couple of years. But I didn't think the costs would be this high for mentorship. I knew I needed to do something about this. That's why, after learning wonders through my own research experience and seeing the frustration of my friend, a female student of color from a first-generation family who yearns to do research, I longed to share this tool for empowerment among my younger peers in my community and around the world.

THE REALITY IS...

Research empowers people to pursue interests and learn a set of practical skills, such as problem-solving, critical thinking, presentation, communication, and more. So it shouldn't be a surprise that there has been a huge demand from students to master the knowledge and skills related to research. For example, each year more than *half a million* middle and high school students in the United States participate in the National History Day contest, which requires students to conduct historical topic-related research.

Box 0.1 National History Day

National History Day, established in 1974, is a nonprofit education organization based in Maryland that is dedicated to improving the teaching and learning of history. Every year, more than 600,000 students around the world conduct original research on historical topics of their choosing and create projects to present their findings.

Source: National History Day, 2023, NHD, https://www.nhd.org/.

The Society for Science, hosting the world's largest international pre-college STEM competition, indicates that more than 1,800 *selected* high school students from around the world submit their STEM-related research during the International Science and Engineering Fair (ISEF).

Box 0.2 The Society for Science

The Society for Science has been dedicated to expanding scientific literacy, access to STEM education, and scientific research for more than one hundred years. Every year, it supports the more than 1,800 high school students from around the world who will be competing for nearly $6 million in awards during International Science and Engineering Fair (ISEF, https://www.societyforscience.org/isef/), the world's largest international pre-college STEM competition.

Source: The Society for Science, 2023, Society for Science, https://www.societyforscience.org/.

This need is seen even in elementary schools when science fairs are hosted. However, in elementary, middle, and often even high schools, it's rare that a research course is offered. No nonprofit organization has accessible research programs designed for elementary to middle school students, which makes getting started in research extremely difficult. There are still so many aspects of research where guidance and mentorship are needed, though, like research methodology, choosing a research topic, staying on task, and more.

IF RESEARCH IS SO DIFFICULT AND ARTIFICIAL INTELLIGENCE (AI) CAN WRITE MY PAPERS, DO I EVEN NEED TO LEARN RESEARCH?

With the recent launch of ChatGPT in November 2022, a powerful new AI chatbot, you may wonder if learning the research skill is still needed or even worth it. It is true that, in a short period of time, Chat GPT has become controversial and there have been many debates about its impact on the future of education. Some want to ban it. Some embrace it as a learning tool. Some of you may think since Chat GPT is far faster in data processing *and* analysis *and* generating essays *and* papers than we humans could ever do, there is no point in learning how to do research.

To understand the value of research, we need to go back to the purpose of it. The purpose of research is not just to get results and conclusions; rather, the emphasis should also be on the whole research *process* and being critical of other literature. This literature includes the answers Chat GPT gives you. What if AI and past studies are wrong? Without going through the research—challenging other theories and findings—we won't have an "aha" moment and intuition to make further progress. As researchers, we have been the key drivers behind innovation and originality in the past. Today's AI tools should only enhance and assist our research and innovation rather than replace them. Our brains should be in the driver's seat. Research skills and ability are the fuel to enable us to remain on that seat and progress far. As *The Human Factor: The Fundamental Driver of Innovation*, a report by the World Intellectual Property Organization (2014), stated,

> *The fundamental driver behind any innovation*
> *process is the human factor associated with it.*

Why is the research process more important than its result? Let us imagine scientists can create a medicine that generates the same amount of tiredness and happiness as you would have after finishing a marathon. Would you just take the medicine and bask in the feeling of accomplishment? You may gain short-term satisfaction, but your muscles would gradually weaken and be incapable of running. When presented with this question, I personally would instinctively say, "No! That is ridiculous."

Do you see how a similar argument can apply when relying on ChatGPT? If one day a machine can do thinking and innovation for us, what is left for human brains then?

As of today, as Stahl (2023) commented, "ChatGPT can write grammatically correct, readable articles solely based on its training data. It cannot generate original content or make editorial decisions."

On the positive side of AI, if managed well, the success of ChatGPT actually proves to us that critical thinking, the most crucial skill that a researcher possesses, will become even more important. With proper and thoughtful control, AI could take the teaching of critical thinking to a whole new level. Critical thinking is about reading, *researching*, being able to differentiate and, at the same time, being open to multiple viewpoints, and being able to organize all the information you collected into something cohesive and understandable with logic and clear structure.

So, yes, AI could become a teaching aid—one that unlocks student creativity, offers personalized tutoring, and better prepares students to work alongside digital technologies. It may create more opportunities to inspire and support young researchers. But ultimately, tools are tools, and we need to learn how to use them—and use them well—instead of letting them replace our precious intuition, creativity, innovation, independent thinking, as well as fun parts of any game. This is why it is even more critical to master the set of practical skills that doing research could train us to do.

SO, MY GOAL IS...

This book aims to address the lack of research support, courses, mentorship, and information for aspiring researchers at the elementary to middle/high school level as a supplement to the K–12 curriculum. Here, I would like to clarify that this book's purpose is not to make anyone a "research expert." It serves to help students who come up with amazing research ideas but don't know where or how to start and don't have the resources to. The mission of this book is to *inspire, support, and empower* the next generation of aspiring young researchers in a vibrant way.

RESEARCH TO EMPOWER

We all like to ask if there is one straightforward answer to a frequently asked question: "How do you become a good researcher?" The truth is, there's no one-size-fits-all way. What there is, however, is a set of steps that can help you get inspired and become interested in finding your *own* way of doing research in a systematic and fun manner.

As young students, when we talk about doing research, we often get scared and feel it is something intimidating. Doing research can be mysterious and even scary! In reality, it is just starting with something small that you are passionate about or interested in. Once you find a project or a problem you feel the urge to solve, think of it like playing a game. It doesn't matter if it's a sport, video game, puzzle, simulation game, or role-playing game. So, in this book, you will learn the rules of the game, refine your goals, choose your "weapon(s)," deal with all the nitty-gritty details and strategies, activate on-the-grind mode, dress up before the victory, share your glory, and even unlock two massive treasure chests.

HOW WILL READING THIS BOOK HELP YOU GET INSPIRED AND HELP YOU START YOUR RESEARCH JOURNEY?

Research to Empower is the embodiment of the best part of my four years of high-intensity research experiences from being involved in fourteen international research projects (as of May 2023) while simultaneously growing from a middle school to a high school student and juggling other extracurriculars. You can say I have seen a lot, been there, and done that! I know how you feel. That is why I would like to present this book in an engaging and illuminating way as a "not your typical How to Research book" for you—young students.

HOW SHOULD YOU READ THIS BOOK?

The "you" I refer to throughout the book is the young student. But this book is also for families, parents, teachers, educators, and administrators who want to use this as a guide for teaching at home, in classrooms, or in any other setting. Finally, of course, this book is for anyone who is interested in starting research! The goal of this book is to promote fairness and inclusiveness in education, after all.

Here is a quick explanation of what the little symbols you'll see throughout mean:

💥 You can do it too!

These encourage you to try it yourself, like following the steps shown or answering critical thinking questions. You can find all these exercises on this digital notebook file if you prefer to fill it out that way. The "treasure chest" at the end has a bunch of links, so it may be easier to click on it through this notebook.

Or, of course, I encourage you to write in and annotate this book to make it truly yours.

💜 Little Nudge.

These are little motivating reminders or suggestions about the mindset to have when approaching a problem.

💡 HINT.

These are key tips for when you are doing research.

If you ever hit a word that is unfamiliar, check out the glossary at the end of this book for your reference.

Let's think of it as playing a fun "game."

Are you ready to get started?

LET THE
GAMES BEGIN!

Chapter 1

Loading... A New World

"Research is creating new knowledge."

–Neil Armstrong (1930–2012),
American astronaut, first man to walk on the Moon

WHAT DO YOU THINK RESEARCH IS?

Maybe the first thing that comes to your mind is something along the lines of "Differential Plasma Entomography for the Classification of Pregenerational Anthroinformatics and Paradynamics of Bionormative Quantum Physics using..."

Don't panic and close the book yet! I made that research project title up with the purpose of making it sound frightening. But you would be surprised to find how many people have the impression that research is exactly this. Actually, every single piece of research can be boiled down to something very simple, something we see or make every day: a question (or multiple ones).

Think about all the times when a random question popped up in your head, like, what type of diet is healthier and more sustainable, vegan or vegetarian? Why do we like social media so much? How did schools originate and who designed them? Is there science behind people preferring milk before cereal or cereal before milk? Is there a way to read books and somehow absorb them faster? (Hey, no cutting corners with this one...) Here, I also selected some of the most bizarre research questions to give you some inspiration (see Box 1.1).

Box 1.1 Some selected bizarre research questions

1. Can people swim faster in syrup or water?

2. What sort of surfaces are the best for dragging sheep?

3. How much surface area does an Indian elephant have?

4. Does highlighting prevent you from understanding what you are reading?

5. Do teenagers pick their noses a lot?

6. Are falling coconuts dangerous?

7. How dangerous are collapsing toilets?

8. What species of Costa Rican tadpole tastes the best?

9. What is the optimal way to dunk a biscuit?

10. Can farting make you feel better?

11. Can chicken feathers be used to determine the speed of a tornado?

12. Does wearing wet underwear make you feel cold during winter?

Source: List25.com, 2022.

Here are three research papers that I thought were interesting. My point is that anything that catches your interest could potentially be your research!

Box 1.2 A few Goodmen: Surname-sharing Economist Coauthors

Title: A Few Goodmen: Surname-Sharing Economist Coauthors

Authors:
Allen C. Goodman, Wayne State University
Joshua Goodman, Harvard University
Lucas Goodman, University of Maryland
Sarena Goodman, Federal Reserve Board

Summary: The paper explores the phenomenon of co-authorship by economists who share a surname. It is the first paper coauthored by four non-related, surname-sharing economists. It examines the various impacts of sharing the same name and further research.

Economic Inquiry ＼＼ WEAI

Miscellany

A FEW GOODMEN: SURNAME-SHARING ECONOMIST COAUTHORS

Allen C. Goodman ✉, Joshua Goodman ✉, Lucas Goodman ✉, Sarena Goodman ✉

First published: 30 October 2014 | https://doi.org/10.1111/ecin.12167 | Citations: 4

Read the full text >   🗋 PDF 🔧 TOOLS < SHARE

Abstract

We explore the phenomenon of coauthorship by economists who share a surname. Prior research has included at most three economist coauthors who share a surname. Ours is the first paper to have four economist coauthors who share a surname, as well as the first where such coauthors are unrelated by marriage, blood, or current campus. (JEL Y9)

REFERENCES   ∨

Citing Literature   ∨

Source: Goodman et al., 2014.

Box 1.3 The Toilet Paper Problem

Title: The Toilet Paper Problem

Author: Knuth, Donald E.

Summary: Using mathematical research, this paper describes that in the toilets of Stanford there are two rolls of paper. Some people stick to using the bigger ones, some people tend to use the smaller ones, and some people will use them randomly. After the paper runs out, some staff replace it with a new one, and when two rolls are all empty, everybody is in trouble.

THE TOILET PAPER PROBLEM

DONALD E. KNUTH
Computer Science Department, Stanford University, Stanford, CA 94305

1. Introduction. The toilet paper dispensers in a certain building are designed to hold two rolls of tissues, and a person can use either roll.

There are two kinds of people who use the rest rooms in the building: *big-choosers* and *little-choosers*. A big-chooser always takes a piece of toilet paper from the roll that is currently larger; a little-chooser always does the opposite. However, when the two rolls are the same size, or when only one roll is nonempty, everybody chooses the nearest nonempty roll. When both rolls are empty, everybody has a problem.

Let us assume that people enter the toilet stalls independently at random, with probability p that they are big-choosers and probability $q = 1 - p$ that they are little-choosers. If the janitor supplies a particular stall with two fresh rolls of toilet paper, both of length n, let $M_n(p)$ be the average number of portions left on one roll when the other roll first empties. (We assume that everyone uses the same amount of paper, and that the lengths are expressed in terms of this unit.) For example, it is easy to establish that

$$M_1(p) = 1, \quad M_2(p) = 2 - p, \quad M_3(p) = 3 - 2p - p^2 + p^3; \quad M_n(0) = n; \quad M_n(1) = 1.$$

The purpose of this paper is to study the asymptotic value of $M_n(p)$ for fixed p as $n \to \infty$. We will see that the generating function $\sum_n M_n(p)z^n$ has a surprisingly simple form, from which the asymptotic behavior can readily be deduced. Along the way we will encounter several other interesting facts.

2. Recurrence Relations. Let us begin by generalizing the problem slightly, using the notation $M_{mn}(p)$ to stand for the mean number of portions left when one roll empties, if we start with m on one roll and n on the other. Thus

$$M_n(p) = M_{nn}(p);$$
$$M_{m0}(p) = m;$$
$$M_{nn}(p) = M_{n(n-1)}(p), \quad \text{if } n > 0;$$
$$M_{mn}(p) = pM_{(m-1)n}(p) + qM_{m(n-1)}(p), \quad \text{if } m > n > 0.$$

The value of $M_n(p)$ can be computed for all n from these recurrence relations, since no pairs (m', n') with $m' < n'$ will arise.

It is convenient to visualize the recurrence by drawing certain arcs between adjacent lattice points in the plane, where the arc from (n, n) to $(m - 1, n)$ has weight p and from (m, n) to $(m, n - 1)$ has weight q, for all $0 < n < m$; the arc from (m, n) to $(n, n - 1)$ has weight 1 for all $n > 0$; and there are no other arcs. Then $M_{mn}(p)$ is the sum, over all $k \geq 1$, of k times the sum of the weights of all paths from (m, n) to $(k, 0)$, where the weight of a path is the product of the individual arc weights.

A path that starts at the diagonal point (n, n) must go first to $(n, n - 1)$; then it either returns to the diagonal at $(n - 1, n - 1)$ or goes to $(n, n - 2)$, etc. Let c_k be the number of paths from (n, n) to $(n - k, n - k)$ whose intermediate points do not touch the diagonal, and let d_{nk} be the number of paths from $(n, n - 1)$ to $(k, 1)$ whose points do not ever touch the diagonal. A path that starts at (n, n) either returns to the diagonal for the first time at some point $(n - k, n - k)$, or never returns to the diagonal at all; it follows that

---

The author is Fletcher Jones Professor of Computer Science at Stanford University. "My main life's work is what I like to call the *analysis of algorithms*, but I also enjoy doing research in supporting disciplines such as combinatorial and discrete mathematics, programming languages, and digital typography."

Source: Knuth, D. E., 1984.

39

Box 1.4 Chicken Chicken Chicken: Chicken Chicken

> **Title:** Chicken Chicken Chicken: Chicken Chicken
> **Author:** Zongker, Dong, University of Washington
> **Summary:** Chicken.

Chicken Chicken Chicken: Chicken Chicken

Doug Zongker

University of Washington

Chicken

Chicken chicken chicken chicken chicken chicken chicken chicken chicken chicken chicken chicken *chicken* chicken chicken chicken chicken chicken. Chicken chicken chicken chicken chicken chicken chicken chicken. Chicken, chicken chicken chicken, chicken chicken, chicken chicken chicken "chicken chicken" chicken "chicken chicken" chicken. Chicken, chicken chicken chicken chicken chicken chicken chicken chicken (chicken chicken) chicken chicken chicken chicken chicken, chicken chicken chicken chicken chicken chicken chicken chicken chicken chicken chicken chicken chicken chicken chicken chicken. Chicken chicken chicken chicken chicken chicken chicken chicken chicken, chicken chicken chicken, chicken chicken chicken chicken chicken chicken chicken chicken.

CC Chickens: C.3.2 [Chickens]: Chicken Chickens—chicken/chicken chicken; C.3.4 [Chicken chicken]: Chicken chicken chicken—chickens; C.2.4 [Chicken-chicken chickens]: Chicken/Chicken, chicken chickens

Chickens: chicken, chicken chicken, chicken, chicken

1 Chicken

Chicken chicken, chicken, chicken chicken chicken chicken, chicken chicken chicken chicken chicken chicken chicken [4]. Chicken chicken chicken chicken, chicken chicken chicken chicken: chicken chicken chicken chicken chicken chicken chicken chicken chicken, (chicken chicken chicken chicken chicken chicken chicken, chicken chicken chicken chicken chicken chicken chicken chicken!)

Chicken, chicken-chicken chicken chicken—chicken chicken, chicken chicken chicken 95% chicken chicken-chicken chicken, chicken chicken chicken chicken—chicken chicken chicken chicken chicken. Chicken, chicken chicken, chicken chicken chicken 1987. Chicken chicken chicken chicken chicken chicken-chicken-chicken chicken chicken chicken chicken chicken chicken chicken chicken chicken chicken chicken chicken chicken. Chicken chicken, chicken chicken chicken chicken chicken chicken chicken chicken (chicken chicken chicken chicken chicken chicken chicken chicken chicken chicken chicken chicken chicken).

Chicken chicken chicken chicken chicken chicken, chicken chicken chicken (chicken chicken chicken chicken chicken chicken chicken) chicken chicken chicken chicken chicken chicken. Chicken chickens chicken chicken chicken chicken "chicken" chicken chicken chickens chicken. Chicken chicken, chicken-chicken chicken chickens, chicken chicken chicken chicken chicken chicken chicken.[1] Chicken chicken's "chicken" chicken chicken chicken chicken—chicken *chicken chicken* chicken chicken chicken, chicken chicken chicken chicken chicken chicken chicken chicken.

---
[1]Chicken chicken chicken chicken *chicken chicken* chicken; chicken chickens. Chicken chicken Chicken [5].

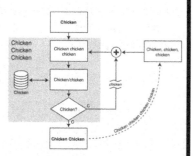

Chicken 1 *Chicken chicken chicken. Chicken chicken, chicken chicken (chicken chicken chicken) chicken chicken-chicken.*

Chicken chicken chicken chicken chicken. Chicken-chicken chicken chicken chicken chicken chicken chicken, chicken chicken chicken chicken chicken, chicken, chicken chicken chicken chicken "chicken" chicken. Chicken chicken chicken chicken chicken chicken chicken, chicken, chicken chicken chicken. Chicken chicken chicken chicken chicken chicken chicken (chicken, chicken-chicken chicken chicken chicken-chicken chicken-chicken chicken-chicken chicken). Chicken, chicken chicken chicken chicken chicken chicken chicken chicken chicken. Chicken chicken chicken chicken chicken chicken chicken, chicken chicken-chicken chicken chicken chicken chicken chicken chicken chicken chicken (chicken). Chicken chicken chicken chicken chicken chicken chicken, chicken chicken chicken chicken, chicken chicken, chicken chicken chicken chicken chicken chicken.

Chicken chicken chicken, chicken chicken chicken, chicken chicken chickens chicken chicken chicken chicken. Chicken, chicken, chicken chicken chicken chicken chicken chicken-chicken chicken, chicken chicken chickens Chicken 2. Chicken chicken chicken chicken chicken chicken chicken chicken chicken chicken, chicken chicken chicken. Chicken chicken, chicken chicken chickens chicken. Chicken chicken chicken chicken (chicken chicken Chicken 3), chicken chickens chicken chicken chicken (Chicken 4). Chicken chicken chicken chicken, chicken chicken chickens chicken, chicken chicken chicken chickens chickens chicken. Chicken chicken chicken chicken chicken chicken.

2 Chicken chicken

Chicken chicken chicken, $C(n)$ chicken chicken chicken chicken chicken chicken chicken [4]. Chicken chicken chicken chicken chicken chicken chicken chicken's chickens Chicken [3] chicken chicken, chicken chicken chicken ch-

Source: Zongker, D., 2002.

Note: This is included for comedic purposes. This paper is actually a great template for reference. I don't recommend submitting something like this to a publisher, though! After all, it's no longer original.

Formal Definition of Research

From the Code of Federal Regulations (45 CFR 46.102(d)):

> *Research is a systematic investigation*
> *(i.e., the gathering and analysis of information) designed*
> *to develop or contribute to generalizable knowledge.*

According to the American sociologist Earl Robert Babbie in the book titled *The Basics of Social Research* (2002),

> *Research is a systematic inquiry to describe, explain,*
> *predict, and control the observed phenomenon. It*
> *involves inductive and deductive methods.*

In simpler terms, research is a detailed dive into a particular subject (using special methods) with the goal of adding to that subject.

So all of the spontaneous questions from before could be turned into a research project if you wanted to! It's like solving a puzzle or a mystery, or beating a game that you've been pondering over for months once and for all.

THERE ARE THREE MAIN PURPOSES OF RESEARCH:

1. **Exploratory:** To investigate a group of questions, especially new problem areas that haven't been explored before. We're venturing "into the unknown!"

2. **Descriptive:** To focus on expanding knowledge of current issues through data collection. It describes the behavior of a sample population.

3. **Explanatory:** To understand the impact of specific changes in existing standard procedures. This usually involves running experiments.

✴ You can do it too!

Circle the type of research purpose that you are interested in!

Exploratory   Descriptive   Explanatory

MY EXAMPLE:

Let's take a trip down my memory lane and look at my first self-initiated research from four years ago.

> **Title:** "Breaking the Barriers in Women's Fencing: Historical Roots, Title IX, and Empowerment of Women"

Key Question: What is the role of fencing in women's empowerment?

Main Purpose: Exploratory.

Photo 1.1 A fencing tournament inspired my first research project

Source: Author, 2023

Photo 1.2 Publication in the Journal of International Women's Studies

Home > Journals and Campus Publications > JIWS > Vol. 24 > Iss. 3 (2022)

Breaking the Barriers in Women's Fencing: Historical Roots, Title IX and Empowerment of Women

Grace Chenxin Liu

Abstract

Fencing, often referred to as a physical game of chess, is an organized sport involving the use of a sword, épée, foil, or saber for attack and defense according to set movements and rules. Fencing, one of the first nine sports included in the first Olympic Games in 1896, has a long history. This paper has systematically reviewed literature and evaluated the role of fencing in the empowerment of women through a combination of qualitative and quantitative research methods including first-hand observation, interviews, archival analysis, and secondary statistical data collection. It has attempted to narrow the empirical gap by exploring the gender perspective of fencing as a sport. It reveals that due to historical, social and cultural bias, financial constraints, as well as a lack of leadership, women's involvement in fencing had been limited throughout fencing's history. Since the 2nd half of the 19th century, fencing has witnessed tremendous strides in breaking the barriers influenced by the changing society propelled by a long history of feminist and civil rights activists who took a blend of the consciousness-raising and organizing approach and the

Source: *Journal of International Women's Studies*, 2022, https://vc.bridgew.edu/jiws/.

~ CHAPTER SUMMARY ~

★ Research is not necessarily all scary, technical language. It can be fun (and involve toilets and chickens…).

★ Research papers basically boil down to their research questions and are a detailed dive into a specific subject using certain methods.

★ There are three main research purposes: exploratory, descriptive, and explanatory.

Chapter 2

A Love Letter to Research: What's in It for You?

"Research is seeing what everybody else has seen and thinking what nobody else has thought."

-*Albert Szent-Györgyi* (1893–1986),
Nobel Prize–winner in Physiology or Medicine in 1937

WHY IS RESEARCH IMPORTANT FOR STUDENTS LIKE YOU?

Research opens a new world for you to not only discover your passion but to also go in-depth and learn incredible new things about this passion. Plus, understanding the process of research dissemination (spreading your work) and publication can lead to expanding your professional networks, which is extremely important for your future and enhancing your lifelong skills. If you are still wondering what the point of research is if AI can just write it for you, stick around for the note at the end.

Let's elaborate on these key points to hit it home!

DISCOVER YOUR PASSIONS

This is the fun and more experimental part of a research journey. It involves getting to know yourself more because you are identifying your areas of interest! Think about the following questions:

- What excites you?
- What questions keep you up at night?
- What do you feel are problems that NEED to be addressed?
- What do you think the future needs?

LEARN NEW SUBJECTS AND ENHANCE LIFELONG SKILLS

Learning how to research is like an all-in-one, deluxe study package. You can...

- Enhance knowledge by getting to know the intricate details about a topic. For example, you may want to understand the subject from scratch—starting with the original studies.

- Clarify confusion about facts and figures to erase any doubt. This is key to becoming an expert!

- Gain confidence in your work and learn how to work independently.

- Get a clearer picture of your future career.

- Learn many valuable skills like problem-solving, time management, professionalism, presentation and communication, analysis, teamwork, quick in-depth reading, and efficient online searches.

RECOGNIZE YOUR WORK: DISSEMINATE, PUBLISH, AND GAIN NETWORKS

This is arguably the most rewarding part because you'll see your hard work finally pay off. It's your turn to see your paper published and be referenced by other researchers! To do so, we'll introduce the dissemination and publication process and go into the details later in this book (see chapters 11 and 14).

When sharing your work, you'll encounter brilliant scholars and potentially work closer with them. You can learn so much from these people, and it's life-changing. Another bonus: you gain academic credentials! This can give you more publishing opportunities. It's like a snowball; once it starts rolling down the hill, it'll only get bigger and faster.

INSPIRE OTHERS AND ADVANCE SOCIETY

Just like the quote from Neil Armstrong in the first chapter, "research is *creating new knowledge*" [my emphasis].

You will inspire others with your original research! Think about the impact you can have on another person if your work can motivate them to join you. It's immeasurable.

The ultimate goal of the research is to understand nature and society better. Without research, humanity cannot propel itself forward. As humans, we are fueled by being curious, asking questions, discovering, and thriving by learning.

A FINAL NOTE ON THE CURRENT EVENTS ABOUT AI

All of the points I just mentioned are the reasons why technology can't replace research. Research is about *asking questions* and understanding *why* we ask questions—it's not completely about the results!

The process of research also involves so much learning, and a robot can't replace that for you. Gaining knowledge is a long-term process that truly results from research, and the results of your paper come from this process along the way. Having AI do research for you may initially save time, but it defeats the core purpose of why most people do research: to ask questions and think critically.

MY LOVE LETTER TO RESEARCH

Dear Research,

Greetings from Grace!

Looking back, these past four years of my journey with you have been the most intellectually challenging, physically tiring, and emotionally draining ones of my life. But they are also the most rewarding and best that I've ever experienced. I'm so proud to have come this far and absolutely ecstatic to scream, "I DID IT!" Throughout this journey, I have found my true passions, which may be one of the most valuable outcomes, through you. I have learned to love you, especially in the interdisciplinary fields of gender studies and sustainable development. It is why I would love to—and am determined to—devote more time and effort in expanding knowledge in gender equality and advancing women's empowerment.

By learning how to confront you, I have also learned and sharpened a set of practical skills such as problem-solving, critical reasoning, thinking in-depth and from different perspectives, presentation and communication skills, time management, working with deadlines, negotiation skills, professionalism, and confidence. And that's why I could not be more grateful for you.

Along the way, I have been honored to have met and made friends with amazing like-minded people, including mentors, teachers, scholars, students, and experts. Some of my best memories are from participating in global conferences to present my research findings. I was able to continue working with other panel members, and we saw the need to promote and support the educational, professional, and personal development of scholars and students who seek to make a change through research and international collaboration. As a result, I was able to create Research To Empower, the first student-run nonprofit organization to inspire and empower the next generation of aspiring young researchers, making research accessible to all, regardless of age, gender, race, or financial background. Can you believe that?

You also taught me how to solve real world problems through collaboration and teamwork. In one international team research project under the theme "Public Health Impacts on Climate Change," I was blessed to work with five talented young researchers to develop a telemedicine app with geographic-specific resources to reduce heat-induced health problems in underserved populations from Miami, Florida called MiHealth. Without you, dear Research, I would have never gotten to meet these amazing like-minded people.

You give me the opportunity to bring value, such as my published research "Breaking the Barriers in Women's Fencing: Historical Roots, Title IX and Empowerment of Women" to society. That research is creative and fills an empirical and theoretical gap in research, can be replicated and built upon, contributes to a better understanding of women's empowerment in sports, aids in overcoming hurdles on the road to women's empowerment, and has the potential for immense social change toward gender equality.

Moving forward, I know that there are still many sleepless nights to be spent with you. But I won't be stopped; I know you will help me with advocacy and deepening my understanding of the fundamental issues I care about *so* much: What hinders gender equality and sustainable development?

Truly, thank you, Research. You have changed my life.

Love,
Grace

🎆 **You can do it too! Reflect on why you want to research.**

Refer to the questions in the "Discover your passions" section and jot down your ideas. Or, you can get a bit crafty and write your own love confession letter to research! Maybe you can make a reminder to revisit this in a couple of years to see how far you have grown.

_____

_____

_____

_____

_____

~ CHAPTER SUMMARY ~

★ Through research, you can discover your passions, learn new subjects, enhance lifelong skills, recognize your work, meet interesting people, and inspire others to advance society. That sounds like a good deal to me!

Chapter 3

The Rules of the Game: Research Ethics

"A man without ethics is a wild beast loosed upon this world."

—ALBERT CAMUS (1913–1960),
French author, philosopher, and journalist

LIKE IN ANY GAME OR setting, we need to know the rules before diving in. In research, these rules are called "ethics."

What are ethics? The word comes from the Greek root *ethos*, meaning "character." What that means for research is that it's important to adhere to moral principles or what's fundamentally right.

But then the question arises...

Why are research ethics important?

Staying ethical is merged into the entire process, from selecting the research problem to carrying out research goals as well as interpreting and reporting research findings. There are several reasons for this, so let's imagine the following *fake* scenarios to show what can happen if we *don't* have research ethics.

1. People pretend to be experts, make up false facts and data, and publish it in a paper—it's chaos! Everyone is suspicious that you're lying...and you're suspicious that they're lying. How can you possibly write a paper like this?

Ethics prevent this from happening by promoting research norms: knowledge, truth, and avoiding error. This way, researchers are held accountable to the public.

2. You want to work with other people in different institutions, so you end up writing a paper together. But, when it's published, you see that your name isn't on it even though you wrote half of it!

Teamwork makes the dream work...but it needs ethical standards for it to work. Ethics ensure researchers receive credit for their contributions and do not have their ideas stolen or revealed too soon.

3. An oncologist injected cancer cells into patients, without their permission, to learn how people's immune systems would react. Although the patient gave consent to be injected, details about the true nature of the experiment— that cancer cells were involved--were kept secret.

Human research is research conducted with or about people, their data, or their tissues with the sole intention to do good. Human research involves significant risks and it is possible for things to go wrong. A real-life example is the famous Stanford Prison Experiment that tested people's psychology by having participants roleplay prisoners or guards. The horrifying thing is that the prisoners were kept in unsafe conditions and the guards started taking it too seriously and abusing them.

Thankfully, this can't legally happen today. But, despite the best intentions and care in planning and practice, sometimes things go awry. Ethics prevent this from happening.

4.   One day, creativity hits you, and you have a brilliant idea for a research project. The only problem is that you lack the funds for it to happen. No one funds research anymore since it's unethical (sad, I know).

Ethics help build public support for research. People are more likely to fund a research project if they can trust the quality and integrity of the research.

With ethics in place, these four catastrophes are usually avoided, phew! Basically, ethical research advocates for moral values—such as human rights and welfare, animal care, following the law, and staying healthy/safe—which is super important not only in research but in society as a whole.

You can do it too! Summarize the DOs (ethical) and DON'Ts (unethical) of research.

Table 3.1 Adaptations from the Society for Science ethics statement

DO this	DON'T do this
• Have integrity by being honest and objective. • Avoid conflicts of interest in every research phase. • Follow all federal, state, and local laws. Projects done outside the US should follow that country's laws. • Respect confidentiality and honor intellectual property.	• Cheat off of people and write that your work is independent when it wasn't. • Use unpublished data or results without giving credit or having permission. • Carelessly throw toxic chemicals, garbage, or invasive species into the environment after experiments.

DO this	DON'T do this
• Protect the environment when doing experiements.	• Play around with substances that can damage your health like Potentially Hazardous Biological Agents (PHBAs). • Violate human participant protection. • Write up bogus data and commit scientific fraud.

Source: The Society for Science, 2022.

Table 3.2 Patton's checklist of questions for conducting an ethical research project

1. Explain the purpose of the research	Accurate & understandable
	Use lay language (no jargon)
	Decide what should and should not be shared
	How will the research contribute to society, their community, the world?
2. Promises and Reciprocity	Don't make promises you won't or can't keep
	Why should the participant take part in the research?
	What's the benefit to them?
3. Risk Assessment	How will this put the participant(s) at risk?
	Could there be legal implications?
	Could the study cause psychological distress?
	If you uncover controversial information, how should it be shared?
	How will you communicate potential risk and handle issues that arise?
4. Confidentiality	What are the commitments that can be honored?
	Confidentiality and anonymity—you either know the identity of the subject but keep it confidential or keep the identity anonymous (not even the researchers know the subject's identity).
	What information will be changed?
	What information can you NOT promise to keep confidential?
	Data storage & maintenance (time and place)

5. Informed Consent	Is it necessary? What kind will work for the situation?
	Institutional Review Board (IRB) guidelines—what are they, how are they followed, and what needs to be submitted to them?
6. Data Access and Ownership	Who will have access and why?
	Ownership of data—who? Communicate this to the participant(s)
	Who (if anyone) can review findings/data/paper before release or publication?
7. Interviewer Mental Health	Will interviewer(s) be negatively impacted by study?
	Could there be a need to talk about the experience? Can this be done without breaching existing contracts?
	How will the interviewer(s) care for themselves?
8. Advice	Who will be the go-to person or persons for the researcher(s) during the study regarding ethics issues that may arise?
9. Data Collection Boundaries	To what extent will you press participants for data?
	Where will you draw the line?
	What if participants become uncomfortable?
10. Ethical vs. Legal	Develop an ethic framework/philosophy
	Go beyond what is required by the law
	Will you have a professional or disciplinary code of ethics as a guide?

Source: Patton, 2002, p. 408.

~ CHAPTER SUMMARY ~

★ Ethics means sticking to what is morally right, which is important because it's integrated into the entire research process.

★ If we didn't have ethics, catastrophic experiments would be allowed and research may lose its credibility.

★ Ethical research advocates for morals like human rights and welfare, following the law, staying healthy/ safe, and respecting each other's work.

Chapter 4

What I Wish I Knew Before Starting

"You should never view your challenges as a disadvantage. Instead, it's important for you to understand that your experience facing and overcoming adversity is actually one of your biggest advantages."

–MICHELLE OBAMA (1964–), American attorney and author who served as First Lady of the United States from 2009 to 2017

THROUGHOUT YOUR RESEARCH JOURNEY, IT is unavoidable that you will be facing challenges—from choosing a topic to staying sane throughout the process, and every step in between.

Jim Jourdane, a French illustrator, interviewed scientists about their everyday mistakes when being biologists, archeologists, entomologists, and volcanologists. He published a book called *Fieldwork Fail: The Messy Side of Science* to tell the stories of scientists working in the field.

From gluing yourself to a crocodile, accidentally peeing on a jaguar's marked tree and being chased by it for three weeks (funny until you actually experience it), swallowing fossils, to having your shoes melted by lava, these stories show some challenges and bloopers of the Researcher "Life in the Dreamhouse."

Remember in the beginning when I said there were many hurdles? Here are some of the major challenges I faced while doing my research projects. I share this with you because it's likely that you'll face some of them too, and I hope this can at least ease your troubles.

♥   **Little Nudge.** Don't be intimidated by all this talk about challenges and hardships and whatnot. Think of this chapter as a vaccine shot; it may sting a bit, but don't let it get in your way of achieving greatness. Then you won't be surprised when these challenges *do* pop up and say hello!

CHALLENGE 1 - CHOOSING THE RIGHT TOPIC

I always find that choosing and finalizing research question(s) and a topic is challenging because simply finding a research topic that is original and suitable for your interests is a tough job on its own.

So, please be super careful with choosing your topic! Your research topic is the foundation of your long-term project, so we want to avoid it collapsing on you when you're only halfway done. Be aware that you should consider your available resources like time, money, and people. Ask yourself: Can I do this topic justice? Do I *really*, from the bottom of my heart, love learning about this? Is this a niche area in which I can make a difference? It's okay if the answer is "um…" or "I don't think so." The next chapter (chapter 5) will detail what you need to know to turn the answer into "YES!! Of course! I have the topic that even Goldilocks would approve of."

CHALLENGE 2 - CHOOSING THE RIGHT METHODS

Once you've chosen a topic, you'll need a research methodology—a procedure for conducting your research—in order to move forward. This usually involves a lot of back-and-forth between different specific methods.

I'll use my first research project, which I mentioned in chapter 1 and was about fencing, as an example. At first, I chose to use only qualitative methods (which don't involve numbers). It seemed logical because I had easy access and the ability to collect primary data (data that comes from first-hand sources rather than second-hand sources such as textbooks). I received saber training at a fencing academy two to three times a week, so I could not only play or observe the sport being played but also have the opportunity to interview my coaches and peers.

As my research progressed, I realized that using only qualitative methods could be unstructured and not rigid enough (more on the pros and cons of each method later in chapter 7). I didn't want a biased or misleading conclusion, so I integrated quantitative methods by searching for data from various sources. Using both qualitative and quantitative methods helped me view the subject in a more dynamic light and understand the reasons behind decisions, behaviors, or actions.

I think this quote from Dr. Linda Crawford, a faculty member in Walden University's PhD program is perfect: "The best way to choose it is not to choose."

You might think, "WHAAAT? Doesn't that go against your whole chapter on choosing a method?" Actually, I interpret this quote as meaning that you should use methods based on the research questions, not solely on what you like doing.

CHALLENGE 3 - SEARCHING FOR HELP

A huge part of research is feedback and talking to people. If you're shy (like I used to be), this might mean the end of the world, but wait! Eleanor Roosevelt once said, "Do one thing every day that scares you."

For every research project, I always write a list of the people around me who could potentially help me and reach out to them either in person or via phone or email. For example, I reached out to my Project Beyond teacher at the time. I also cold-emailed more than one hundred researchers and scholars in my field—not only in the USA but also in the UK—to see if they were interested in my topic and would like to provide initial feedback on my proposals. At an early stage, my Project Beyond teacher helped me fine-tune my research topic. After every discussion and exchange of ideas with him and other people I could reach, I would make updates to my research based on their feedback and the lessons I learned. Although the process was tedious and time-consuming, I could see my research progressing with my key research questions and areas I would focus on shaping up nicely.

Another example is finding participants for my interviews to collect data for my first research project. I wanted to interview my coaches who were teaching my saber classes. I knew that all of them were extremely busy, and I was also still a nervous and shy kid at that time. But I went ahead anyway, and all four coaches turned out to be very supportive of my research.

Looking back, if I had listened to my fear, I never would have completed my project and gone so far with it. At that time, my parents were telling me: "Just go for it—the worst thing that can happen is people say no. *And so what if they do?*" It's true; it isn't like I was physically harmed when people said no. At least I tried and did not regret it.

💜 **Little Nudge.** Reaching out to people, especially if you need mentors and participants for your study, may be out of your comfort zone. Some institutions may be unfriendlier than others. But that's okay; you're not alone, and we all go through it. As an old saying goes, "Where there's a will, there's a way!"

CHALLENGE 4 - WORKING IN A TEAM

Oftentimes, you need to work on a team—which is fun—and you can be more productive and creative when you put your minds together. This is obviously amazing, because, at some point, when the novelty of research wears off, you don't want to be stranded somewhere alone. Having a team is like going for a really long run, but you have friends by your side to chat with you, take your mind off the frustration, and—look!—before you realize it, the finish line is already there. Time sure does fly when you're having fun!

Having a support group can be like a ray of sunlight through endless gray clouds. Personally, I'm forever grateful for my family and how much love they give. For you, it could be friends, family, teachers, and whoever you feel comfortable with. Ranting about all your troubles, even if it's to a wall, can be therapeutic! I'm definitely guilty of doing that.

I have worked on more than ten international research teams with team members and/or mentors from Brazil, China, Egypt, Germany, India, Papua New Guinea, Portugal, Saudi Arabia, Spain, Tunisia, the Philippines, the United Arab Emirates, the United Kingdom, and the United States...and *whew, there is a lot more to it than what meets the eye!*

There is handling the different time zones, communication issues, understanding cultural differences, and learning to appreciate different perspectives. This last point is a very important trait of good researchers.

Try to join a team of teammates and mentors who are responsible and have a good track record of being able to deliver what they are supposed to do on time.

☀️ **HINT:** Read their biographies and make note of their geographical location and expertise. If possible, request a quick chat with them to see if they are ready to commit. Doing your "homework" will avoid a lot of problems down the road.

Once your team is formed, you need to make sure that everyone knows exactly what the team's goals and deadlines are and what their own individual goals are. If you are leading (go you!), I suggest not micromanaging everyone's tasks, because great leaders are flexible enough so that the work is done and the members are all happy with what they've contributed.

🔅 **HINT:** Use tools like Google Calendar, Google Sheets, Slack, Notion, Taskade, Trello, or anything else you find. Those are free, and I have personally used them and found them to be friendly, collaborative workspaces. There are many paid programs and packages like Microsoft 365 that you can also consider exploring.

When I worked on "Space Power" for the Flexible Use of Electricity global challenge, I teamed up with five other people from Brazil, India, the Philippines, and the United Arab Emirates under the supervision of Dr. Garret Schneider, our mentor from the New York Academy of Sciences. We worked the "old-fashioned" way—using a table to keep track of all the documents and deadlines we had. Now, as I mentioned, there are a bunch of software and apps that can help you do that. It's up to your team to decide what everyone is more comfortable with, but definitely write your plans, track tasks, check them off when completing them, and leave notes for other teammates to follow up on. Our project findings ended up being featured on the United Nations SDG Learncast podcast!

Photo 4.1 Group photo of the Space Power team

Source: The UN SDG Learncast, 2022.

Photo 4.2 Interview by The United Nations SDG Learncast

Source: The UN SDG Learncast, 2022.

CHALLENGE 5 - STAYING MOTIVATED

The beginning high and enthusiasm wear off. You face rejections and lose motivation just like many of your peers and researchers before you. You might begin to think, "Is this even worth it? Maybe I should give up. I don't want to do this anymore."

No! This is when you should remind yourself of the reasons why you started in the first place.

♥ **Little Nudge.** Don't stop at the first, second, or even third rejection. There are always other avenues to do things; it's just a matter of persevering.

It may help to take a couple of days off as a break, if time permits. When I hit a block, sometimes the only way to break through is by leaving it alone for a couple of days and letting it dissolve a bit on its own. When I come back, there are always many things I see that I missed before, and it becomes easier to jump back into the research project with a pair of fresh eyes.

If you are tighter on time, a short break still helps. Personally, developing a habit of exercising or getting in at least a bit of physical activity every day has been life-changing. It's great for your health and career because it's a perfect way to destress and unwind so that you can come back to your project stronger.

I used to go swimming and fencing two or three times a week until the pandemic because my school district's swimming facility and my fencing club closed temporarily. Later, I found my love for running when I joined my school's cross-country team. On school days, I take a twenty- to forty-five-minute break after finishing homework. On weekends, I run for thirty to sixty minutes after a couple hours of work in the afternoon. This is a typical routine that I still stick to today, even as I write this! My most recent goal is to prepare and try for a full marathon in 2024.

Photo 4.3 Successful completion of my first Icebreaker Half Marathon for Medals 4 Mettle Long Island, January 29, 2023

Source: Author, 2023

You don't have to start out like this, and I'm not trying to say my routine is the best; it's just what works for me and my schedule. Even a five-minute walk might help you clear your head after stressful hours of sitting at a desk. If you're artsy, you can take a brain break by doodling for a bit.

THE ULTIMATE CHALLENGE...PROCRASTINATION (AND OTHER TOXIC FEELINGS WE KNOW ALL TOO WELL)

Let's face it—it's tough to balance a lot of things on your plate. With school grades and clubs (plus the drama that comes with them), after-school activities like sports and competitions, and trying to have a social life, it can be a lot already. And now you want to add *research*!?

Take it easy. It helps to remember the importance of using your time wisely and knowing that time is scarce, because once it's spent, there's no getting it back.

💜 **Little Nudge.** At the same time, don't go crazy with guilt for spending time outside of research or other important things, especially if it's for a good reason. I used to feel ashamed after I spent an hour on a Saturday night laughing on the living room couch and watching TV with my family, because my mind was telling me, "You should be working on research!" or "You could be doing more meaningful things right now!" I hope you don't experience this. My point is that it is up to your judgment when deciding the extent of how much you will plan out your schedule. My general suggestion is to plan but not micromanage, especially if you're a perfectionist like me who might get stuck making sure the plan is perfect but unable to execute.

It helps to start by creating a timeline with milestones for a project and breaking it down into smaller tasks. In fact, my biggest piece of advice is to start small. As James Clear, author of *Atomic Habits*, puts it, "Make it easy to start and the rest will follow…. Start by mastering the first two minutes of the smallest version of the behavior."

I used this concept of the "Two-Minute Rule" to start and complete research projects that took months or years. As a full-time student, I used my after-school hours, weekends, holidays, and summer breaks to work on my research projects. This included a lot of things (see the list below), but I kept in mind the principle of just getting started instead of worrying about how long each of these projects would eventually take.

Table 4.1 A sample timeline of breaking down research tasks

General Goal	Day-to-Day, Small Task
Learning necessary knowledge and skills.	Open up a textbook and block out a time on my calendar to study.
Reviewing literature and finalizing the key research questions.	Read one journal article at a time and take note of the key ideas.
Drafting and finalizing the research plan/proposal.	Block out a time to just write! Start with a first sentence.
Communicating with mentors and teachers.	Email/message them the moment you have updates (so you don't forget later).
Collecting primary and secondary data.	Complete this just for section X of the paper.
Analyzing data.	Complete this just for section X of the paper.
Drafting the research paper and report.	Write it up one sentence at a time.

Disseminating my research findings.	Explore different opportunities, apply for conferences, and post on social media.
Submitting and revising for internationally peer-reviewed journals.	Revise the paper section by section, if needed.

Source: Author, 2023.

Photo 4.4 A sample to keep track of the milestones and timeline for a research project

Source: Author's calculation, 2021.

Please note that this is just a sample. Work at your own pace given your circumstances! Also, honestly, this was before I discovered all of the shiny, cool productivity apps. I encourage you to experiment with those instead of tracking everything on Excel to see if you like the app's design better.

✵ You can do it too!

Create your timeline.

Goals	**Target finishing date**	**Time Period it took (fill this in after you complete the goal)**
Start date		
Topic chosen		
Literature reviewed		
Proposal done		
Done with data		
First draft of paper written		
Feedback requested		
Paper revised (according to comments)		
Disseminated (submitted to journals)		
Other milestones		
COMPLETED!!		

~ CHAPTER SUMMARY ~

★ Beware! There are many challenges (and potential pitfalls) like choosing the right topic, searching for help, staying motivated, and procrastinating.

★ Going out of your comfort zone, reminding yourself of your "why" for research, having a support group to team up on this marathon of a research journey, and just getting started on your plan are strategies to undertake hurdles.

Part Two

GAME-IN-PROGRESS

Chapter 5

3...2...1...Blast Off!

"Well begun is half done."

–Aristotle (384–322 BC),
ancient Greek philosopher and polymath

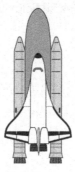

NOW THAT YOU'VE GOTTEN YOUR feet wet and understand what research is, why you should do it, the rules of research, and some things to be cautious about, it's time to get started! Grab a seat, grab a snack and some water, and relax! It's time for the fun to begin.

PICK A (BROAD) STUDY AREA

This is like choosing the type of game that you want to play. Is it a puzzle or a board, computer, virtual reality, sport, or multiplayer game? Just like playing chess is drastically different from playing Pac-Man, different major study areas will take you on a very different path.

According to Cambridge University Press, there are seven categories of major study areas:

1. Clinical Medicine

2. Life Sciences

3. Humanities and Social Sciences

4. Business and Law

5. Physical Science

6. Engineering and Materials Science

7. Mathematics and Computer Science

There are many, many topics under each category! This multitude of topics is like the specific game modes and variations, and under each mode, there are different "players" or "strategies" that you can choose.

As a simpler and less technical example, let's look at the Humanities and Social Sciences, which have eight modes: communication, education, arts and humanities, public policy, economics, political science, information management, and social and behavioral sciences. Each of these branches out into even more specific topics. Since, unlike an actual game, the research covers so much, even these specific topics are pretty general.

Table 5.1 Categorization of Humanities and Social Sciences

Communication	Education	Arts & Humanities	Public Policy

Cultural Studies
Journalism
Media Studies
Public Relations
Publishing/Media
Scientific
   Communication
Technical
   Communication
	Educational
	   Administration,
	   Policy and
	   Leadership
	Educational
	   Philosophy
	   and Theory
	Educational
	   Psychology
	Educational Research,
	   Curriculum and
	   Instruction
	School Counseling
	Special Education
		Architecture,
		   Design
		   and Planning
		Art History
		Behavioral
		   Geography
		Classical Studies
		Cultural Studies
		Gender Studies
		History
		Linguistics
		Literature
		Music
		Philosophy
		Religious Studies
		Theatre Studies
		Women's Studies
			Agricultural
			   Economics
			   and Policy
			City Management
			   and Urban Policy
			Environmental Policy
			Health Policy
			International Relations
			Other Public Policy
			Public Administration
			Social Policy

Economics	**Political Science**	**Information Management**	**Social & Behavioral Sciences**

Agricultural
   Economics
   and Policy
Behavioral Economics
Development
   Economics
Econometrics
Economic Theory
Environmental
   Economics
Health Economics and
   Outcomes Research
International
   Economics
Macroeconomics
Microeconomics
Other Economics
	American
	   Political Science
	Comparative
	   Political Science
	International Relations
	Other Political Science
	Political Theory
		Information
		   Retrieval and
		   Management
		Library Science
			Anthropology
			Archaeology
			Behavioral Geography
			Behavioral Economics
			Criminology
			Marketing
			Nursing
			Psychology
			Social Work
			Sociology
			Urban Studies

Source: Cambridge University Press, 2023.

WHAT ARE YOUR PASSIONS AND INTERESTS?

Don't worry if you can't answer this now. Believe it or not, this is a difficult question many people struggle with! You may have absolutely no clue, and that's okay. Or, you may have some inklings of ideas right now that are too broad. For example, if you know that you like computer science and Google "research on computer science," you will get an overwhelming amount of information and articles.

That's why I'm here to help you narrow down your topic, so that it goes from what seems like an ocean of information to a single cup of water! We're taking a huge boulder and carving, sculpting, and whittling it down to a clean, small, precise, beautiful work of art.

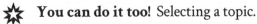 **You can do it too!** Selecting a topic.

Try some or all of these prompts and, in the end, review your response to see if there are topics that have shown up more than once. Are they closely related or linked?

☀ **HINT:** Think about what you have experience with! Maybe it's something that you have done for many years.

Find a newspaper with a wide variety of topics. Try looking through the many articles and, without overthinking it, open or highlight all the ones you would like to read.

Summarize it: What types of titles capture your eye most often?*

_____

_____

_____

_____

_____

*Feel free to use the seven major study areas!

What classes are your favorite? What makes them interesting? What unexplained phenomena still baffle you?

_____

_____

_____

_____

_____

What are your hobbies, personal interests, or extracurricular activities? Can you find a related question or problem that can be researched from your personal experiences?

_____

_____

_____

_____

_____

MY EXAMPLE: HOW I GOT STARTED AND WHAT INSPIRED ME

Title: "Breaking the Barriers in Women's Fencing: Historical Roots, Title IX, and Empowerment of Women"

Looking back, I can connect the dots of what inspired, influenced, and motivated me to pursue this research project. I didn't really consciously know it back then because I didn't have a guidebook like this one to tell me what I should do, so I went more with the flow.

Based on what you know so far, let's play a little guessing game where you guess what three main things inspired me. This is mini-practice for when YOU reflect on yourself when the time comes, which is important because you can understand yourself better. It also helps to reconstruct a researcher's thought process as an example for your research.

Write down your predictions here.

_____

_____

_____

_____

Photo 5.1 Fencing training at Island Fencing Academy, 2019

Source: Author, 2019.

The first inspiration is obvious: **the fencing classes** I took! This was a personal interest and extracurricular activity of mine. I attended Island Fencing Academy in New York. For over a year of my life, I lived and *breathed* the possibility of becoming a skilled fencer worthy of national competitions. I'm blessed to have been a student learning from amazing coaches Maksim Lahotska, Boris Khurgin, Misha Shimshovich, and Brittany Cubano. I'll never forget them or their lessons.

I had never considered myself an athletic person. I used to view sports as chores to keep myself healthy, so I did the bare minimum...until fencing. Fencing taught me how to love a sport and how to be eager to get fitter. I looked forward to every class and was exhilarated after every practice. Fencing changed me. I learned how to recollect myself after failing and I didn't realize how much of a confidence booster that could be. At the time, we had to do timed fitness tests, including one for running. I didn't think much about it, hoping to get through half of it at best. I ended up being the only girl to last through the entire thing, breathing heavily but not winded like the others who were rushing for water. The sensation that rushed through me was none other than joy and "whoa, I didn't know I could do this. I can't believe I proved myself *and* others wrong." I saw how much fencing impacted me and wondered if I could see impact in other people too by addressing gender inequality and discrimination through my research!

If your guess was something along the lines of "something I read" or "something I heard," you're right! The second inspiration was **one of the speeches by Nelson Mandela**, the former president of South Africa, at the inaugural Laureus World Sports Awards. He said:

> *Sport has the power to change the world. It has the power to inspire. It has the power to unite people in a way that little else does. It speaks to youth in a language they understand. Sport can create hope where once there was only despair.*

I saw this during my literature review and it sparked my interest to read more. I noticed how existing literature on fencing was mainly focused on the history of fencing, fencing techniques, psychology of fencing, health-related issues of fencing, or biographies of fencers. There wasn't any research into the gender bias perspective of fencing, which made me even more curious and led to my research questions.

The third inspiration can be traced to **my love for history and global issues during my childhood days**. At the time, I would refer to global issues as "adult stuff" because they seemed like abstract concepts but intrigued me nonetheless. Throughout my life, I've always enjoyed late-night discussions at the dinner table about the latest international news. I spent most of my weekends as a child reading at the local public library or browsing the internet about related topics. I always had a feeling of satisfaction after sharing knowledge with others—and now. I feel honored to pinpoint and share knowledge with you!

When I was ten, my mom was the one who first encouraged me to do research. Obviously, I was bewildered as someone who believed the myth that research was only done in fancy, scary, too-complicated labs. She told me to try to learn how to conduct quantitative and qualitative research and, along the way, explore what my passion was. Just like that, my research journey began in 2019.

NARROWING DOWN YOUR INTEREST INTO A SUBTOPIC

Here come the stages where you whittle your interests down. These are some methods to identify a specific problem/question to address:

1. **Read and review journal articles, books, or websites:** What do you notice is *not* covered but you would like to see?

2. **Observe your everyday life:** What is a difficulty you want to help fix that can be applied on a wider scale?

3. **Look at things with a different lens:** What is another perspective on a broad topic? How can you combine multiple topics to intersect at a unique, niche area?

4. **Ask a teacher or expert:** What have they written about and why? What do they think is a good study area that has the potential for future impact?

CHOOSING A RESEARCH QUESTION

You have to be a bit nitpicky with this and assume the role of Goldilocks. Your question, which is your final research topic, should be very specific. It should have some details—like what you are targeting or perhaps a specific place or location you are studying—because global research can be extremely broad and difficult to go in-depth.

But it can't be *too* specific. If your question is filled with too many details of who, what, when, where, and how, you'll find yourself able to answer it in one quick answer or number, and then we'll have a problem: there's practically no research that you can do!

✳ **You can do it too!** Choosing your research question/topic.

Which method did you use to narrow down your topic during the stages of whittling it down? (This can help you write a section called Methodology. *wink wink*)

_____

_____

_____

_____

_____

What is your research question?

_____

_____

_____

_____

Let's double-check it (to avoid getting stuck in Challenge 1)!
Is your research question **FINER** (Cummings et al., 2013)?

- **F**—Feasible (do you have the resources to do it?)

- **I**—Interesting (do you *actually* want to do it?)

- **N**—Novel (is it new, unique, or innovative?)

- **E**—Ethical (see chapter 3)

- **R**—Relevant (oof...this is brutal, but will others care?)

Are you...

- Unable to answer the question in a quick sentence? If you are able to give a yes/no or one-sentence answer, the question may be too specific and needs revising.

- Able to answer the question without having to write ten books on it? If you do need to write that much because the population you consider is too large or there is too much to be written for you to be thorough, the question is too broad.

Reflection time: Does your question fit these guidelines? If not, can you add to or subtract from your question to define it further?

_____

_____

_____

_____

_____

💜 **Little Nudge.** This is *not* easy! Don't worry if you feel that you are progressing slowly. This first step can take a long time and feel frustrating, but know that you *can* solve your problems and get through the obstacles on your research journey. It will make your life easier if you get this beginning part right, just like the quote at the beginning of this chapter from Aristotle!

MY EXAMPLE

It all started with a simple observation: "I love fencing, and ever since I started fencing, I felt confident about myself."

Okay, I knew I wanted to write about fencing and gender, but it still wasn't specific enough. After reviewing and reading existing literature (see chapter 6), I specified my topic to "What is the role of fencing in women's empowerment? What are the factors from a historical perspective?" Bingo! My research area was FINER.

I wanted further feedback to be *absolutely* sure if the topic and questions were fine. I reached out to my Project Beyond teacher and experts in this field to fine-tune my research topic. After every discussion and exchange of ideas with them, I would make updates to my research and write reflections/summaries of the key lessons learned. Yes, it's tedious, but it's a solid way to make progress!

Eventually, I found that sports are places where discrimination against women and male domination are broadly considered reasonable and acceptable. This is *why* studying from the perspective of gender bias is not only one of the most important sport-related studies but also one of the most under-researched, especially in the sport of fencing.

Here were my **final research questions:**

- What are the reasons for women's lack of involvement in fencing throughout history?

- How has Title IX promoted women's involvement in fencing since the 1970s?

- Is there a framework that can illustrate and assess the empowerment of women, with fencing as an enabler and driver, that could be applicable, replicated, and built upon for other sports with broad-range and global implications?

Figure 5.1 A flowchart of how to formulate research questions

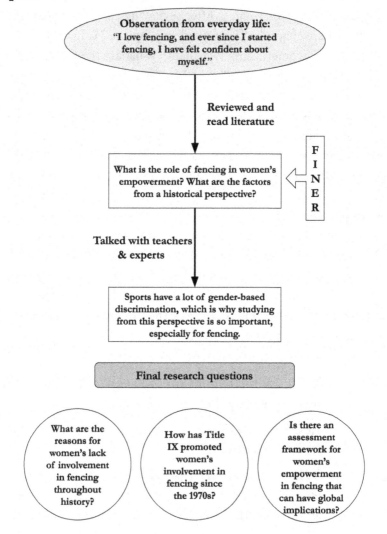

Source: Author's summary, 2023.

SETTING YOUR RESEARCH OBJECTIVES (GOALS!)

Research objectives help us identify what you want to focus on in your research. These are the basic questions that you try to answer in your paper. What do you plan on investigating and evaluating?

This is also where you talk about how important your research is! The questions includes...

1. What is the problem you try to solve and why is it important?

2. What is the exact information you will use to create your new ideas and observations?

3. How will you research (what methods will you use to evaluate your information in an efficient way)?

✳ **You can do it too!** Setting research objectives.

Here is some space for you to jot down your initial objectives. Remember: What problem do you see, what information will you use, and what methods will you use to get that information?

_____

_____

_____

_____

_____

_____

_____

_____

_____

_____

WHAT'S THE HYPE ABOUT HAVING A RESEARCH MENTOR?

Technically, you can complete research without a mentor and do it by self-learning. But to *really* make sure your research is not only high-quality but also goes in-depth, you need someone who has many years of experience in the subject.

Not convinced? Well, mentors are like an all-you-can-eat buffet of knowledge. They...

- Provide access to a lab, full-text journal articles (that you usually have to pay for!), and other resources

- Share experience on how to do good research (including tips and know-how)

- Explain difficult concepts, which saves time and mental energy from frustration

- Provide insight about what is *really* good research in the field (they're insiders, after all!)

- Ensure you don't interpret results or articles incorrectly since it would be painful to find out the day of a research fair/conference or your work not be published because of a silly mistake

- Help with accessing different opportunities or options for your future research

- Help with planning strategic actions and considering various channels for sharing your work

- Give an expert's view on the potential consequences, both positive and negative, of every step along the way

- Recommend new learning tools, methods, and resources (including their priceless advice) for personal growth

- Use their professional network to help out, like looking for feedback or publishing opportunities

WHERE'S WALLY (THE MENTOR)?

Just like the puzzle hunt game, you're on a worldwide search for a mentor. This is like a thick jungle to navigate through. A wrong step could be costly, especially for your time! Let me guide you through.

1. Apply for a summer/winter research program, preferably at a program located in a university where you can interact and connect with professors directly.

HINT: Don't stray off the path! Remember what general topic you are pursuing and stick to it. If your finalized focal point and topic is on the history of art, it's generally a good idea to *stick to* art-related programs.

2A. Hooray! You are accepted into the program. Now, you need to get to know the faculty at the institution better. Ask around, do some background online searches, and see if a professor is interested in mentoring a student or has an ongoing project they need help with.

HINT: Look for people who have been judges in a previous research competition, written articles in your field, or are on the scientific committee of a conference you want to present at.

2B. Maybe you are tight on time or can't find a good program yet. No worries! Mentors don't have to be local unless you *need* to work in their lab to do your project. Emailing or periodically meeting online works too!

💡 **HINT:** It's super important to show how much you love the work you want to do. It makes sense that professors, who are incredibly busy, want to work with dedicated, hardworking, and passionate students. Show them what you've got! Let your nerdiness and enthusiasm shine through!

Other ways to find Wally (your mentor)

- The hard, painfully-looking-one-by-one way: cold-emailing. I cold-emailed over a hundred scholars and experts in the field of gender studies, global studies, and sports studies for my first research project. If you do the same, you'll probably get roughly two to five responses—on a good day.

♥ **Little Nudge.** Don't stress out if this is the only way that would work for you. Although this is tiresome, there's no prerequisite that stops you from starting today! Even one or two responses are better than what you started out with: none.

- Use who you know to help. See if your parents have connections or friends at the local university. For many self-initiated researchers I know, that was how they found mentors.

- Get into a program that does the hard work for you. I reached out to the researchers through the databases of the two international programs I'm in (see The Junior Academy and 1000 Girls 1000 Futures programs in chapter 12). Through them, I had the opportunity to work virtually on six international research projects with mentors who are STEM professionals from all over the world. There are a ton of other programs, in-person or virtual, and opportunities that you can explore in chapters 12 and 13.

💡 **HINT:** This is particularly important if you want to work in a scientific lab! You may see that this book doesn't delve into how to do lab research, and you may have reacted by thinking, "Wait, I thought you would be representative of research! Where's a huge part of research that I happen to love?" This is because your mentor and the possible textbooks your mentor recommends will give you better guides that are practical and comprehensive. Also, a gentle reminder that this book is meant to be an introduction and quite general so that it is easier for you to read!

~ CHAPTER SUMMARY ~

★ Start out with identifying a broad study area by thinking about your interests and how they relate to the seven major area of study categories.

★ As a personal example, my research was inspired by my experience as a female fencer, President Mandela's speech, and my early childhood's broad range of reading and in-depth discussions with my parents. Looking back, those were my interests.

★ Narrow down your general interest into a subtopic by reading literature, observing what's around you, thinking from different perspectives, or consulting an expert.

★ Double-check if your research question is good with the FINER acronym and being Goldilocks!

★ Set some research goals and have a "proposal" in mind when reaching out to research mentors.

★ Mentors can give you an "all-you-can-eat buffet's" worth of resources and guidance.

★ Find a mentor by applying for a research program, cold-emailing, or using your personal networks.

Chapter 6
The Hunger Reading Games: Literature Reviews

"What do researchers know? What do they not know? What has been researched and what has not been researched? Is the research reliable and trustworthy? Where are the gaps in the knowledge? When you compile all that together, you have yourself a literature review."

—JIM OLLHOFF, PHD., educator in social psychology and ethics

THE READING GAMES AREN'T AS extreme as the Hunger Games; they aren't literal death matches against other people...but they're pretty fierce! Similar to looking for edible food for survival and putting it all in your bag, you want to find as much relevant literature as possible and store them in a place you can find. You may want to prepare several places for sorting purposes. Just like someone would avoid eating poisonous berries, we also want to remove irrelevant articles.

WHAT IS A LITERATURE REVIEW?

According to Elsevier's Author Services (2022):

> *A literature review is a study—or, more accurately, a survey—involving scholarly material, with the aim to discuss published information about a specific topic or research question. Therefore, to write a literature review, it is compulsory that you are a real expert in the object of study.*

Basically, it's an overview of the literature on a specific subject, which involves finding, organizing, and making sense of the research. It describes and objectively evaluates scholarly articles, books, and other sources relevant to a particular field of study, helping readers gain a full understanding of the topic at hand.

But do I really need to write about it? Isn't that super tedious? Can't I just keep this to myself and go on with writing my research?

Typically you need a literature review of some sort in your paper. But you raise a valid point...

WHY IS A LITERATURE REVIEW NEEDED?

People might say it's established that any paper should have a literature review of some form. But it goes deeper than that because it:

- helps provide background context for the reader (who we assume has no prior knowledge) on what has already been studied

HINT. Background context explains how your study fits into existing research and why it's important! A typical reason for the importance of a research topic is that it has not been studied extensively in past research.

- ensures that you're not duplicating existing work

- shows your in-depth understanding and knowledge in this subject

- gives an overview of how knowledge has changed in a field

- justifies how your research fits into a larger field and didn't just come out of nowhere

- helps formulate your research questions

- examines the strengths and weaknesses in previous papers

💡 **HINT.** Examining strengths and weaknesses helps you determine your methodology so you don't fall into the same traps as others did! Just like the saying by Warren Buffet, "It's good to learn from your mistakes. It's better to learn from other people's mistakes."

✦ **You can do it too!** How to search for literature.

1. Define your literature review sources. This can include, but isn't limited to:

    a. Scholarly books

    b. Scientific papers

    c. Conference proceedings

    d. Established schools of thought

    e. Relevant articles from specific scientific journals

2. Define your source selection criteria.

    a. What is the range of publication dates that you will include?

    b. Will you focus on a specific geographic region?

    c. Will you only include articles that used a specific methodology?

    d. What are the keywords that you plan to use?

3. Look for articles in libraries, online databases, and reference lists of other reviews or recent articles.

💡 **HINT.** Don't forget, the article should be relevant to your topic! This also means that if you define a time range to study, the article should be within that range. If you don't have a specific time period, try to find more current and up-to-date ones.

4. Read the selected articles thoroughly and evaluate them.

   a. Which articles are the most relevant and useful or most important?

💡 **HINT.** Key articles' references help you to identify other useful references–basically giving you a reading list to add to your own list.

   b. What are the common findings?

   c. What are the trends in the research?

   d. What are the most influential theories?

   e. What are the general pros and cons?

💡 **HINT.** The cons lead to why your research questions are so important and can address the shortcomings.

You can start by writing your answers to this directly in your paper draft or outline!

SOME OTHER POINTS TO REMEMBER...

What happens when you need to look for online websites or sources? Typically, scholarly books and peer-reviewed papers are credible and reliable. But can the same be said for your every-day website?

Hopefully, your first instinct is to be skeptical! One of my technology teachers once told me he saw a Wikipedia article that had some completely false information, and he knew because he's a professional working in the field. On the other side of the coin, sites like Wikipedia are not always bad, and they can often be a handy-dandy resource because their reference lists can lead you to related, peer-reviewed papers. Like with all online websites or articles, though, be cautious!

A rule of thumb: if the article has references or an "About Us" section that explains it is an established organization for providing facts, it should be okay to use. If you see websites ending in ".gov" or ".edu," it means you are on a government or university website, which is generally trustworthy.

💜 **Little Nudge.** If, right now, your head is spinning with all of this information, slow down. Take a deep breath. This is *not* done in one day! Literature reviews can be a long process where you continuously add to your list of references and papers.

If you have already found a bunch of papers and are having trouble referencing back to find the ones you need, now is a good time to find a way to organize all of the literature you come across. Even the ones you toss out for the sake of your paper, keep them somewhere else (in a folder, listed in a document, or any other way) for future reference. This will become your personal research bookshelf and database. You will be able to find not only the literature itself but also your own notes about your intuition even many years after you complete this research, and that knowledge stays with you forever. In fact, my research mentor told me that the world's top researchers are either good at memorizing or staying organized. It's very rare to find someone with both traits. Through training, at least you can develop a good trait of staying organized on your way to becoming a top researcher!

Let's say you're following this plan, avoiding false information by being critical of things you read, and everything is running smoothly. Suddenly, you read several articles and hit a terrible brick wall.

WHAT HAPPENS WHEN ARTICLES CONTRADICT EACH OTHER?

Or worse: What happens when you read a paper written by a Nobel Prize laureate or a world-famous professor while writing your paper and it contradicts *your* conclusions and intuition?

Chances are, you'll react like me and have a sick feeling (*literally*, I once caught the flu after reading a paper that had the opposite results of my paper). You might be tempted to throw out your precious work in a fit of rage, angry at life for slapping you in the face just when things were going well. You may want to throw your intuition out the window while you're at it, thinking, "Gosh! How could I have been so silly? Of course, the Nobel Prize winner is right and *I'm wrong*. Time to rewrite my whole paper!"

Stop right there! Hold all your negative thoughts! And keep your intuition too. What if your initial reaction is wrong? *Both* your intuition *and* the expert can be right. Here's why.

During your first read of a paper, you haven't taken the time to let things sink in, notice all the important details, or think deeper about what the author means. It's normal; scientific literature can have a truck-ton of information in your face at first. It's possible that you interpreted the author's findings incorrectly. Maybe the results aren't relevant to your paper at all. Maybe the setting of the experiment doesn't even match the setting of your research question.

:'Q': **HINT.** A key part of literature reviews is to read key papers several times, often waiting a couple of days or weeks before revisiting them. Each time, you are likely to discover a whole new level of understanding and clearly see some key bits that you may have missed before!

Whatever it is, don't let go of your ideas on how to analyze your results, because that is the core of the paper. It can be difficult not to be completely swayed by a paper, and this is why you need to think critically about whether or not a paper matters (and not just superficially) to your research.

MY FIRST EXAMPLE

Following the "How to search for literature" steps…

Title: "Breaking the Barriers in Women's Fencing: Historical Roots, Title IX, and Empowerment of Women."

Sources: books, academic journal papers, monographs, and newspapers.

Selection criteria:

- Time range: N/A.
- Geographic region: global.

- Specific methodology: N/A.
- Keywords: gender in sports; women's empowerment in sports; women's fencing; history of women's fencing; Title IX.

Where I found literature: academic databases such as ScienceDirect, Google Scholar, JSTOR, and ProQuest; reports from the United Nations, the International Olympic Committee, and other international databases.

After reading and evaluating...

- Common findings, trends, and themes: Existing literature on fencing has mainly focused on the history of the sport; the specifics of the fencing technique, the psychology, injury prevention, and health-related issues of fencing; types of fencing weapons; and biographies of great fencers.
- Findings: Although it is recognized that gender bias in sports is important, there is a lack of research from this perspective on fencing as a sport.

MY SECOND EXAMPLE

Title: "The Gender Digital Divide: A Review and Future Research Agenda from a Feminist Perspective"

Sources: books, academic journal papers, monographs, and newspapers.

Selection criteria:

- Time range: published between 2010 and 2021.
- Geographic region: global.
- Specific methodology: N/A.
- Keywords: Gender inequalities; digital inequality; literature review; gender sustainable development; feminist approach.

Where I found literature: ScienceDirect, ProQuest, Sage Journal, JSTOR, EconLit, Google Scholar databases, and research from international organizations.

After reading and evaluating...

- Common findings, trends, and themes: Existing research can be categorized into three categories: 1) The determinants of the gender digital divide, namely mobile phone ownership; socioeconomic factors, stereotypes, and other root causes; availability and participation in information communication technologies (ICTs) and the internet; and e-government; 2) The impacts of ICTs and bridging the gender digital divide such as positive effects on sustainability, gender equality and empowerment of women, the economy, education, and politics; 3) The regional perspective consisting of case studies on specific regions and countries.

- Findings: There is no literature review on this important topic (the gender digital divide) from a feminist perspective. There is a lack of change-seeking or definite policy implications in these studies.

Figure 6.1 Literature selection procedure

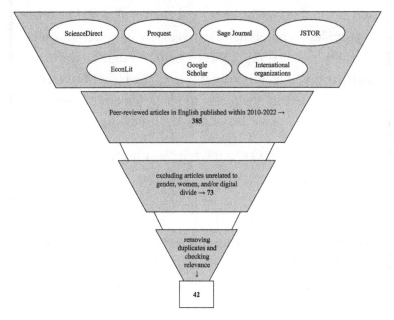

Source: Author's summary, 2022.

AN EXCERPT FROM MY LITERATURE REVIEW

Systematic reviews are a way to find and synthesize all existing research on a subject (Scheerder et al. 2017). According to Tranfield et al. (2003), although this credible, meticulous method can be more tedious than traditional reviews, it provides a comprehensive overview of research topics. Furthermore, it is replicable by being straightforward and trustworthy, which is why it was applied (Lythreatis et al. 2022). Drawn from the systematic review method (Tranfield et al. 2003), this paper undertook the following three steps:

- Step one: Outlining and planning the review,
- Step two: Performing the review,
- Step three: Writing the review.

During step one, the plan for this review was formulated after careful consideration of the research topic. For this particular research, the topic is to provide a feminist perspective in literature reviews for future researchers to consider in gender digital divide studies, especially in the aspect of policy recommendations and future research agenda. Then, a thorough outline, including a list of precise keywords to search, the inclusion/exclusion parameters, and a list of resources (e.g., databases and journals) was written for a clearer direction. This procedure was determined ahead of time to avoid any possible bias and confusion during the process. Additionally, establishing the inclusion/exclusion practices eliminates unfairness from potential preconceived ideas and ensures high-quality selected papers, which strengthens this review (Vassilakopoulou and Hustad, 2021).

During step two, conducting the research put the plan created in step one into action. Firstly, the selection of the timeframe is based on how more research into the gender digital divide has emerged in the past decade. Secondly, to ensure fair coverage of related research, the author searched six widely used multidisciplinary academic research databases, namely ScienceDirect, Proquest, Sage Journal, JSTOR, EconLit, and Google Scholar databases in the field. Research from international organizations, such as the eleven UN organizations and Organisation for Economic Co-operation and Development (OECD), were also included since they notably carry out reliable and comprehensive studies. The author browsed for full-text publications from the selected databases including articles, books, and book chapters—excluding conference proceedings, book reviews, theses, commentaries, letters, and short surveys. To identify the literature to be reviewed, the author searched for "gender digital divide" in the abstract, title, or keywords within databases.

~ Chapter Summary ~

★ A literature review is an overview of the literature on a specific subject that finds, organizes, and makes sense of the research to provide a comprehensive understanding of the topic.

★ These are needed because they provide background context, show your understanding of the subject, justify the importance of your work, and help formulate your research.

★ Search for literature by 1) defining your sources; 2) defining your selection criteria; 3) looking for articles in libraries and databases; and 4) reading the selected literature and evaluating them. See my two examples for how to go through with this.

★ Two key tips: 1) Be careful with online websites or articles and spend some time testing them before you trust them; and 2) Create a personal research bookshelf or database of the literature you find with your notes in it. It will help to be organized and remember things down the road.

★ If you happen upon articles that contradict each other or contradict your intuition, don't panic! Think deeper and see if you interpreted the author's findings/setting wrong.

Chapter 1

Choose Your Weapon(s): Research Methodology

"The power of statistics and the clean lines of quantitative research appealed to me, but I fell in love with the richness and depth of qualitative research."

–BRENÉ BROWN (1965–), American professor, bestselling author, and inspirational speaker

LET'S RECAP: AT THIS POINT, you know what your research topic is and you've launched this research project. You know how to do a literature review and may have even gotten through some of the Reading Games barehanded.

It is time to choose your weapons for the rest of the battle. This is what you will use to not only guide you but also for you to "master" how to use it. The reason we need to carefully ponder over which to choose is that you need to be strategic and think about what would work best for you and your research questions. You can't just randomly use something you think is cool but is totally irrelevant to what you're studying (but hopefully what you end up using is fun, too).

Research methodology refers to systematic procedures or techniques a researcher uses to ensure that the study achieves valid, reliable results (Jansen & Warren, 2020). There are three general choices for you to wield: qualitative, quantitative, and mixed methods.

QUALITATIVE METHODS

This is comparable to the softer skills during a battle—more talking and describing, less hardcore technical stuff. Imagine you are on a mission to infiltrate an evil king's realm and get as many opinions on a new product as possible by befriending people. Your ability to talk your way through a conversation can't really be represented by numbers. Don't underestimate this, though!

The Sage Handbook of Qualitative Research (2005) explains it this way:

> The word qualitative implies an emphasis on the qualities of entities and on processes and meanings that are not experimentally examined or measured [if measured at all] in terms of quantity, amount, intensity, or frequency. Qualitative researchers stress the socially constructed nature of reality, the intimate relationship between the researcher and what is studied, and the situational constraints that shape inquiry. Such researchers emphasize the value-laden nature of inquiry. They seek answers to questions that stress how social experience is created and given meaning. In contrast, quantitative studies emphasize the measurement and analysis of causal relationships between variables, not processes. Qualitative forms of inquiry are considered by many social and behavioral scientists to be as much a perspective on how to approach investigating a research problem as it is a method.

Example: How language interprets subjects' beliefs, experiences, and behaviors (Pathak et al., 2013).

The four most common qualitative methods include

1. participant observation
2. in-depth interviews
3. focus group discussions
4. case studies

Participant observation is a method where you are immersed in the day-to-day activities of the participants in your experiment. The objective is usually to record observations under the widest range of possible settings.

In-depth interviews are ways to collect data and information that involve getting *really up-close* (and sometimes personal) with participants. You are meeting one-on-one with them, which can be in person or over the phone.

Focus groups are "a carefully planned series of discussions designed to obtain perceptions on a defined area of interest in a permissive, non-threatening environment" (Krueger and Casey, 2000, p. 5). They're like interviews or guided discussions, but with many people at a time and often for the purpose of looking for feedback.

Case studies are, according to *Understanding Case Study Research*, "small scale research with meaning." You examine particular, complex instances under certain contexts. This should provide an overall holistic analysis. For example, there are case studies done on various specific countries for how a problem affects them individually.

Table 7.1 Qualitative Methods: PROS vs. CONS

Pros	(Possible) Cons
■ Gives rich, detailed data that leaves the participants' perspectives intact	■ Generates different conclusions depending on the researcher's perspective
■ Provides multiple contexts for understanding the subject	■ Is difficult to replicate
■ Creates descriptions based on primary data, which may be easier to understand for people without background knowledge	■ Increases the chance of ethical dilemmas that undermine the overall validity of the study because of use of human subjects
■ Obtains a realistic view of the world that cannot be categorized or understood in numbers/statistics	■ Can be time-consuming and expensive
■ Can develop flexible ways to collect, analyze, and interpret data	■ Can lack data consistency and reliability because the respondent can choose to withhold information
■ Responds to local situations, conditions, and needs of participants	■ Can hinder useful generalizations to make broad policy recommendations due to small sample sizes

QUANTITATIVE METHODS

Let's stick with the story where you are on a mission to find information in an evil king's territory to understand the citizens' rating of a company's product. A quantitative approach would involve more specific measuring and quantifiable "hard" skills. You would need something like the ability to design a survey and operate a robot that knocks on every citizen's door asking to rate the product out of ten.

Obviously, I made that up. A more rigorous definition of quantitative methods by Babbie (2010) and Muijs (2010) is:

> Quantitative methods emphasize objective measurements and the statistical, mathematical, or numerical analysis of data collected through polls, questionnaires, and surveys, or by manipulating pre-existing statistical data using computational techniques. Quantitative research focuses on gathering numerical data and generalizing it across groups of people or to explain a particular phenomenon.

Example: Examining the relationship between body weight and the amount of water consumed.

Table 7.2 Quantitative Methods: PROS vs. CONS

Pros	(Possible) Cons
▪ Allows for a greater number of subjects and generalizing of results	▪ Can have a false representation of certain groups if data is generalized
▪ Is more objective and results have greater accuracy	▪ Results provide less detail on behavior, attitudes, and motivation
▪ Can be replicated, analyzed, and compared with similar studies	▪ Provides numerical descriptions rather than detailed narratives
▪ Can summarize vast sources of information and make comparisons across categories and over time	▪ Often carried out in an unnatural, artificial, controlled environment that produces "laboratory results" instead of "real-world results"
▪ Personal biases can be avoided by keeping a distance from participating subjects and using accepted computational techniques	▪ Preset answer choices (in a survey) may not accurately reflect how people feel

Table 7.3 Qualitative vs. quantitative data

Qualitative data (categorical)	Quantitative data (numerical)
Feelings such as happiness	Age
Religion	Length
Marital status	Height
Native language	Weight
Social class	Income
Qualifications	Size
Types of instruction	Test score
Methods of treatment	Percent
Type of teaching approach	Number of errors
Problem-solving steps	Hours
Personal account of an experience	

Note: Qualitative data can be indexed to be converted into values that represent it. For example, having a scale for the degree of happiness.

MIX AND MATCH: A COMBINATION OF QUALITATIVE AND QUANTITATIVE

Using a combination of qualitative and quantitative data can improve an evaluation by ensuring that the limitations of one type of data are balanced by the strengths of another. It helps to gain a holistic picture and gain deeper insight into particular questions.

This still isn't a one-size-fits-all solution because, for your research project, it may not make sense to use interviews (qualitative), or, vice versa, collecting a large amount of numbers (quantitative) may not fit.

✸ **You can do it too!** Choose your research method.

First, answer some of these prompts:

- "The problem is…"
- "It is an important issue because…"
- "The purpose of this study is …"
- "I can help to fill the gap of knowledge by…"

_____

_____

_____

_____

_____

Now, think about the following factors. Count the number of checkboxes for each column at the end to see which method is the best fit for you.

Qualitative	Quantitative
☐ Your question is "how" or "why" ☐ Your question has keywords like "explore," "understand," and "generate" ☐ You're trying to describe or explain something in words ☐ Your results are not extremely precise ☐ You want to use narrations, stories, and other more subjective responses ☐ You do NOT need numbers!	☐ Your question is "what" ☐ Your question has keywords like "compare," "relate," or "correlate" ☐ You want to test hypotheses or theories ☐ Your information is precise and objective, meaning that it cannot be changed by personal feelings ☐ You want to use calculations, surveys, controlled experiments, and other ways to gather data ☐ You DO need numbers!
TOTAL:	TOTAL:

If you have an equal (or near equal) number of checked boxes for both qualitative and quantitative methods, consider using a mix of the two.

MY EXAMPLE

Title: "Breaking the Barriers in Women's Fencing: Historical Roots, Title IX, and an Assessment Framework for Women's Empowerment"

Method: A combination of qualitative and quantitative research methods.

The reason: Going back to my key questions, they involved "what?" and "how?." I wanted to describe and explain something as well as compare and relate concepts. I needed narrations/stories, but also numbers.

How I used this method: For the qualitative method, I collected information during 2019 and 2020 to understand concepts and experiences for in-depth insights into fencing issues. I made *participant observations, interviews, and archival analyses* of secondary data.

As a female saber fencer, I was a competitive member of the US Fencing Association, so I could experience fencing in its natural setting. I worked closely with four coaches and received saber training. Of the three male coaches, one is a former national men's saber coach at the Junior and Cadet World Championships. Another is a former head coach of a national saber team as well as a certified referee for the World Championships and Olympic Games. The third is a former head coach of a national fencing team. The one female coach is saber fencer who once qualified for the Olympic Games.

I interviewed them to help me better understand the history and barriers of female fencing. As insiders, the coaches' personal experiences, views, and observations enriched my knowledge of the obstacles and the reasons behind those obstacles. It also allowed me to collect valuable firsthand information.

For the quantitative method, I obtained data from the International Fencing Federation, the International Olympic Committee, the Museum of American Fencing, the United States Department of Justice, USA Fencing, and more.

The data helped me to view the research subject dynamically, reflect it on a wider population, and understand the reasons behind decisions, behaviors, or actions.

~ Chapter Summary ~

★ There are three general methods: qualitative, quantitative, and a mix of both.

★ Qualitative involves collecting and analyzing data WITHOUT numbers, such as participant observations, interviews, focus groups, and case studies. This method is great as a realistic and flexible way to collect information but not so great for consistency and generalizations.

★ Quantitative involves collecting and analyzing NUMBERS to look for patterns and relationships and make predictions. This can be through secondary data, surveys, lab experiments, and questionnaires. This method is great for representing a large number of people and accuracy but not so great for "natural" results.

★ A combination of the two can balance the strengths of both but isn't a one-size-fits-all solution.

Chapter 8

The Nitty-Gritty Data
(and How to Deal with Them)

"Above all else, show the data."

–*Edward Rolf Tufte* (1942–), American statistician
and professor emeritus of political science, statistics,
and computer science at Yale University

YOU ARE STILL ON THAT mission to survey citizens' ratings of a product in an evil king's territory. Your robot has collected the data for you, but now it's up to you to make sense of it and present your findings to the queen. Your competitor is using qualitative methods and is skilled in analyzing data, so you must do your part carefully!

Let's take a deeper look into a crucial part of research: data analysis.

WHAT IS DATA ANALYSIS?

It's a process of gathering, structuring, and interpreting qualitative or quantitative data to understand what it represents.

Empirical data is data that has been collected by researchers through observation, experience, or experimentation (Bradford, 2017). This is important because empirical data is considered objective, unbiased evidence.

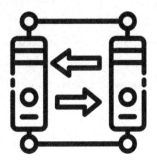

DATA ANALYSIS TOOLS

There aren't any mainstream tools for processing and analyzing qualitative data. Generally, you would have to do things manually when looking for patterns or trends—an eyeball analysis!

Quantitative data analysts and scientists have a variety of special tools up their sleeves to gather and analyze quantitative data from different sources. Google Analytics is just one example of the many quantitative analytics tools available for research professionals. Other quantitative data tools include:

- Microsoft Excel
- STATA
- R
- Python
- Tableau

These tools can have a learning curve, meaning that it takes time to learn and be comfortable with using them. That's the brunt of the work, and I can't provide detailed how-tos for each one because that can be five textbooks on its own. If you have access to video platforms like YouTube, there are many great comprehensive tutorials to get you started.

If you want to work in a scientific lab, you usually would be supervised by a mentor who can teach you the tools, methodology, and data analysis.

MAJOR STEPS FOR ANALYZING QUALITATIVE DATA

Qualitative data analyzers—I hope you didn't think I would leave you hanging! Think of the acronym "VEO CAR" to remember the six steps: validate, edit, organize, code, analyze, and report.

> **Step 1:** Validate. You need to find out, as far as possible, whether the data collection was done as per the preset standards and without any bias. This includes four sub-steps.

> 1. **Fraud:** Was each participant actually interviewed? If you planned on interviewing ten people but only got to five, you can't write that you interviewed ten because that would be a lie.

> 2. **Screening:** Does each participant fit the preset criteria for the target group?

> 3. **Procedure:** Was the data-collection procedure followed correctly?

> 4. **Completeness:** Did the interviewer ask each participant *all* the questions?

Step 2: Edit (applicable to both quantitative and qualitative methods). Large datasets may contain errors. I'm going back to the example surveying citizens of a kingdom using a robot. The robot can't ensure that each person fills in the field correctly and doesn't accidentally skip any questions. So, when you get the dataset back, there could be some blank spaces or totally wacky answers. This is why you should check the data for outliers and edit it to clear out data points that can harm the accuracy of the results.

Step 3: Organize and plot. A classic method of structuring data is to plot all the data you've gathered into a spreadsheet.

Step 4: Code. Although this sounds fancy, coding in this context is just labeling and organizing your data. This way, you can extract meaningful insights and identify issues and the relationships between these issues.

Step 5: Analyze. The task of uncovering insights is to scour through the patterns that emerge from the data and draw meaningful correlations from them. This is about explaining how the evidence you found is relevant to your research questions, intuition, and why it is important.

Step 6: Report. The last step of analyzing your qualitative data is to document the results, to tell the story based on the results. At this point, the insights are developed and the focus is on communicating the narrative to the reader. The next chapter will elaborate on how to do this.

MY EXAMPLE

Title: "The Gender Digital Divide: A Review and Future Research Agenda from a Feminist Perspective"

1. **Validate:** This part was double-checking and triple-checking the papers to make sure that I had everything I needed and that they all fit my research context.

2. **Edit:** In this case, I did this with step one.

3. **Organize and plot:** As you can see below, this was putting all the information on a spreadsheet. The table at the end is the final product though, and during step three, it looked a lot messier.

4. **Code:** I classified the literature into categories and subcategories by reading the abstract and skimming through each paper to garner an understanding of the specified research topic and findings.

a. While doing this, I extracted and noted the author, year of publication, journal/book/ chapter, context (i.e., focused country or region), methodology used, data source (e.g., primary, secondary, or both), and theories/ concepts covered.

5. **Analyze:** I looked at the theories/concepts covered to search for patterns and repeated themes in the keywords. I determined three categories: determinants of the gender digital divide, impacts of ICTs and bridging the gender digital divide, and the regional perspective.

   a. This step of analyzing and looking for patterns shed a clearer view of the subcategories.

   b. The first contained mobile phone ownership, socioeconomic factors, stereotypes, root causes, availability and participation in ICTs and the internet, and e-government.

   c. The second included positive effects on sustainability, gender equality, empowerment of women, economy, education, and politics.

   d. The third consisted of case studies on specific regions and countries such as Latin America, the European Union, Sub-Saharan Africa, and India.

6. **Report:** I wrote this up in the "Findings" section by summarizing each category's research findings. Then I interpreted the reasons for the findings and a critique from a feminist perspective, answering what the research covered (pros) and failed to address (cons).

Table 8.1 A list of selected papers

Author	Publication Year	Journal/Book/Chapter	Context	Method	Data Source	Theories/Concepts
Abu-Shanab, Emad, & Ali Jamal, Nebal	2015	Gender, Technology and Development	Jordan	mix (quantitative	primary (survey))	E-government; gender digital divide; ICT
Abu-Taieh, Evon	2014	International Journal of Social Science & Interdisciplinary Research	International/Global (162 countries)	quantitative	secondary	gender digital divide; social media; effect of literacy rate, GDP, and country location
Acilar, Ali	2020	International Journal of Public Administration in the Digital Age	Turkey	quantitative	secondary	gender digital divide in e-government use; historical trends and differences; gender gap in Internet use; literature review; factors contributing to the GDD
Acilar, Ali, & Sæbø, Øystein	2021	Global Knowledge, Memory and Communication	International/Global	qualitative	secondary	gender digital divide factors; ICT access and use; literature review
Alozie, Nicholas O., & Akpan-Obong, Patience	2017	Development Policy Review	Africa	mix (quantitative and	primary (survey) and secondary	gender digital divide; gender policy; ICTs
Ancheta-Arrabal, Ana, & Pulido-Montes, Cristina, & Carvajal-Mardones,	2021	Education Sciences	Latin America	mix (quantitative and	secondary	gender digital divide in ICTs and education
Antonio, Amy, & Tuffley, David	2014	Future Internet	Developing countries	qualitative	secondary	gender digital divide; digital literacy; education; developing
Bala, Shashi, & Singhal, Puja	2018	Journal of Information, Communication and Ethics in Society	India	quantitative	primary	first and second order of digital divide; internet availability and use
Brännström, Inger	2012	Government Information Quarterly	2 low-income economies in Sub-Saharan Africa	quantitative	secondary	communication technologies; gender; human development; information science; Sub-Saharan

Source: Author's collection, 2022.

~ *Chapter Summary* ~

★ Data analysis is the process of gathering, organizing, and interpreting qualitative or quantitative data.

★ Examples of tools for quantitative data (that may have learning curves): Google Analytics, Microsoft Excel, STATA, R, Python, and Tableau.

★ The six major steps for analyzing qualitative data follow the acronym "VEO CAR":

   1. **V**alidate to eliminate biases and errors

   2. **E**dit the qualitative OR quantitative dataset

   3. **O**rganize and plot on a spreadsheet

   4. **C**ode them (organize and label)

   5. **A**nalyze by uncovering insights, patterns, and connections

   6. **R**eport the narrative

Chapter 9

Activating On-the-Grind Mode and Writing It Up

"I write to discover what I know."

–*Flannery O'Connor* (1925–1964), American
novelist, short story writer, and essayist

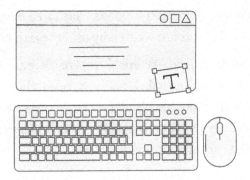

WHY ARE WE SUDDENLY "ON the grind," you may ask? This is typically a tedious part that involves sitting down with your nice, hot cup of tea or coffee, taking a deep breath, and getting to work by typing and writing.

This is similar to a video game when you're trying to level up and, oftentimes, have to go through some repeated actions. Spoiler alert: this isn't even the most tedious part! The *really* repetitive stuff is in chapter 10, but that doesn't take super long. It's all worth it because you will level up, share your glory, and unlock a massive treasure chest soon.

♥ **Little Nudge.** If you've made it this far already, don't forget to give yourself a pat on the back and celebrate!

TYPES OF RESEARCH OUTPUTS

Research outcomes can take many forms such as:

- Books—authored research published by a publisher or self-published.

- Chapters in research books—authored research, often other chapters are written by other researchers.

- Journal articles—refereed before being published in a scholarly journal. Usually, a researcher needs to go through a double-blind review process, which means that both the reviewer and author's identities are concealed throughout the review process.

- Research reports or working papers—usually affiliated with a research institute, university, organization, or think tank.

- Conference publications—usually a researcher registers and attends an academic conference and presents their initial research findings. After the completion of the conference, the researcher may submit the full-length research paper that they drafted. Then, the conference compiles and organizes these papers from each researcher to make the conference proceedings for publication.

- Creative works—like infographics and posters.
- Curated public—like exhibitions and events.

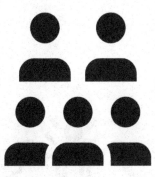

WHO WILL BE YOUR AUDIENCE?

Considering your audience before writing can help guide your writing style. It's simple. Ask yourself: "Who are the readers? Who may take actions on or be affected by the problem of the research?" It helps to envision the audience's age range, gender, education level, economic status, social status, values, and other factors. Next, ask yourself: "What will my readers expect from my writing? How will I keep them interested?"

✦ **You can do it too!** Identifying your target audience.

Who will be affected by what you are researching? Are you writing to the general public? If so, make sure to avoid too much technical language and concepts!

_____

_____

_____

_____

_____

Envision your target audience! Doodle a picture. ☺

WHAT IS YOUR STORY?

Every research paper has a story behind it. It may be what inspired you to pursue it, or it can center around a specific research finding. Sometimes, it can be about weird problems you encountered when implementing the methodology.

When you write your paper or report, try to infuse some of the story's essence. Even in formal journal articles where you will be required to be concise, detailed, and precise at the same time, a good "storyline" can help make an otherwise boring report interesting to the reader.

STRUCTURE OF YOUR PAPER

Although this isn't strict and you'll see a lot of scientific papers published in what looks like a completely different format, most papers contain most or all of the following sections:

1. Title page (including author[s] contact information)
2. Abstract
3. Main body
   i. Introduction
   ii. Literature review
   iii. Methodology
   iv. Findings
   v. Discussion
   vi. Conclusion
4. Acknowledgments
5. References
6. Appendices

✺ **You can do it too!** Reading and annotating a research article

When you are reading the following explanations of each section, have a published research article next to you and highlight (preferably in different colors) the parts that serve a certain purpose. For example, identify the central problems or questions in the abstract and highlight them blue.

I can't include a full-length paper (not even my own!) in this book, because it would be plagiarism. If you want a free and open-access article, you can download either of my full-text papers online:

"Breaking the Barriers in Women's Fencing: Historical Roots, Title IX and Empowerment of Women"

"Financial Flows to Promote Technology Transfers and Gender Inclusiveness for Small Island Developing States"

"Determinants, Impacts, and Regional Perspective of the Gender Digital Divide: A Review and Future Research Agenda"

I don't want you to get lost in the mass of information in the next pages, so welcome aboard to the Train(-ing Your Research)!

The first stop is the Title Station.

The **title page** is the land of first impressions. Here you'll see many researchers taking their time to ponder their titles. Why? Because a title can be a part of the split-second decision that a reader makes when deciding if they want to read your work.

But what makes a good title? Remember the three S's:

1. **S**uccinct (not lengthy or wordy)

2. **S**pecific (the reader should have a crystal-clear idea of what you are writing)

3. **S**ymbolic (it represents your research well and is clearly linked to your research questions)

Typically it should mention these points:

- The broader area of the research, which is the over-arching topic

- The specific focus of your research, also known as your specific context

- Indication of research design (does it have keywords that suggest if your method was quantitative, qualitative, or mixed?)

All aboard! Next stop: Abstract Avenue.

An **abstract** in a nutshell is...a nutshell. It is a short summary of your (published or unpublished) research paper, usually about a paragraph of 150–300 words long. A well-written abstract serves multiple purposes:

- Let readers get the gist of your paper quickly so they can decide if they want to read your full paper

- Prepares readers to follow the detailed information, analyses, and arguments in your full paper

- Helps readers remember the key points and takeaways

Additionally, many search engines and bibliographic databases use abstracts and titles to identify key terms for indexing your published paper. What this means is your abstract and title are crucial for helping other researchers find your paper.

Here is the typical information found in most abstracts. Each point might be a sentence or two:

- The brief context or background information of your research, which includes the general and specific topics you studied

- The central questions or statement of the problem your research addresses

- What's already known about this question? What has previous research done or shown?

- The "why," also known as the rationale and the goals for your research

- Your methodology for researching and analyzing

- Your main findings, results, or arguments

- The significance and implications of your findings or arguments

Next stop: The Igloo of Introductions.

An **introduction** needs to be cool.

...Yes, I acknowledge that joke was not cool. But it doesn't make sense to use "Isle" or "Island" to describe introductions!

They should be interesting and address the importance of the topic. Here are some tips for how to do this:

- Start with a strong opening hook like a statistic or eye-catching fact
- Your mission is to guide the reader into your topic and establish your ideas
- Lead the reader from a general subject area to a particular field of research
- Summarize the current understanding and background information about the topic
- State the purpose of your work and your hypothesis, questions, or researched problems
- Explain your rationale:
    - Why is it important to address these questions?
    - Are you examining a new topic?
    - Why is that topic worth examining?
    - Are you filling a gap in previous research?
    - Are you applying new methods to take a fresh look at existing ideas or data?
    - Are you resolving a dispute within the literature in your field?

The list of questions can go on....

- Briefly explain your methodological approach, highlighting the potential outcomes your study can reveal
- Describe the remaining structure of the paper

- For example: "The structure of this paper is as follows: in Section 1, we introduce.... In Section 2.... Section 3 is the conclusion...."

Next stop: The Reading Games.

Here are the grounds where you would toil through "The Reading Games" I described in chapter 6.

Literature reviews need to cover literature that is important to the issue you are writing about. This can include the key sources that inspired your paper in general or your methodology. This also makes other peoples' lives easier because you collected, summarized, synthesized, and analyzed existing research for them.

☀ **HINT.** Be sure to reference papers properly because this isn't your own work (see chapter 10)! Let's avoid plagiarism.

Literature reviews can be organized in different ways depending on what you are trying to accomplish with the review. Here are some examples:

Chronological: The simplest approach is to trace the development of the topic over time.

Thematic: If you have found some recurring central themes that you will continue working with throughout your piece, you can organize your literature review into subsections that address those themes.

Methodological: If you draw your sources from different disciplines or fields that use a variety of research methods, you can compare the results and conclusions that emerge from different approaches.

Theoretical: In many humanities articles, the literature review is the foundation for the theoretical framework. You can use it to discuss various theories, models, and definitions of key concepts. You can argue for/against the relevance of a specific theoretical approach or combine various theoretical concepts to create a framework for your research.

Next stop: The Shed (of Tools/Weapons).

Research methodology is not just about describing your data-gathering process and your analysis. It's also about why you took the approaches and your perspective during the whole process. A typical methods section should do the following:

Introduce your methods—is it quantitative, qualitative, or a mix of both? Check out chapter 7 again if your memory is fuzzy.

Establish why your methods are relevant—this proves that you didn't pull your methods out of a magic hat; rather, you really thought about how it would be appropriate for your research's objectives. How does it help you when addressing the problem?

Introduce your instruments—what did you use to collect your data? How did you use them? Your tools can be your surveys, questionnaires for interviews, or observations. If you used archival research or analyzed existing data, make sure to give credits to who the original researchers were, background information for documents, and how the data were originally created and gathered.

Discuss your analysis—how will you analyze the results of your data-gathering process? Will you use statistical analyses with fancy technical programs or explore theoretical perspectives to support your explanation of observed behaviors?

Next stop: Field of Findings.

The research findings are like the crops you collect after choosing your tools in the Shed. It represents the core findings of a study derived from the methods applied to gather and analyze information. It presents these findings in a logical sequence without bias or interpretation from the author, setting up the reader for later interpretation and evaluation in the Discussion section. It breaks down the data into sentences that show its significance to the research question(s).

Basically, instead of a huge dataset of numbers or what looks like a million lines of information, researchers present their data and findings in a way that is digestible for readers. You can do so in many ways, such as:

- Data presented in tables, charts, graphs, and other figures
- A contextual analysis of this data explaining its meaning in sentence form
- Specific statistics that correspond to the central research question(s)
- All secondary findings (secondary outcomes that popped up or subgroup analyses)

If your study has a broad scope, used a lot of variables, or yielded a wide range of different results, you should only present the results that are most relevant to the research question stated in the Introduction section.

Next st— Wait! Let's reflect for a bit before moving on.

Discussion of your findings is like the soul of your paper. Here is where you interpret and describe the significance of your findings in light of what was already known about the problem. You use what you know to explain your new understandings and fresh insights.

This should connect to the introduction (where your research questions and hypotheses are) but shouldn't just repeat or rearrange it. It should explain how your study has moved the reader's understanding of the problem forward from where you left them at the end of the introduction.

Next stop: The Closing Circle.

Conclusion is the section where you go back to your main points to summarize them and, if appropriate, make new research suggestions. Watch out; this isn't an exact copy of the introduction or abstract! Just as the introduction gives a first impression, the conclusion makes a final impression and leaves your reader with ideas to think about.

Here is also where you could point in different future directions that could have significant implications. It is where you reflect and be honest about the problems that you encountered and practical limitations that could affect your data. It's always good to spot your errors and acknowledge them before a referee has to do that for you.

Final stop: Thank the driver, give credit, and dump information here if needed.

Acknowledgments give you an opportunity to say "Thanks!" to people who helped you along your research journey. Generally, it's optional, but it's a nice thing to do for people like:

- Your research mentor(s), tutors, advisors;

- Any professors, lecturers, or teachers who helped you understand the topic or methodologies;

- Your editor(s) and anonymous reviewer(s);

- Any institutions, organizations, foundations that financially supported you or provided you with in-kind support;

- Your family and friends; and

- Anyone else who ran the research marathon with you!

Citations and references

Every research builds on previous research—even if it's in a new field, related studies will have preceded and informed it. In peer-reviewed articles, authors must give credit to this previous research through citations and references. Not only does this show clearly where the current research came from, but it also helps readers understand the content of the paper better.

Citations need to be consistent and accurate, typically following one specific style. The next chapter will go into those details.

When you go through your paper to edit or proofread it, look closely at the citations within the text:

- Are they all the same and follow the same format?

- Are they all complete?

- Do they match your references list? (Meaning, you aren't missing any references that you wrote in-text, and you also don't have extra ones in the references that you *didn't* refer to.)

Appendix

This is the part of a paper that contains materials and references that may be very detailed and too much to include in the actual paper or research report.

For example, this can be calculations, mathematical proofs, technical drawings, graphs, diagrams, flowcharts, raw data, tables, maps, photographs, computer programs, musical composition samples, interview questions, and sample questionnaires. This content needs to be summarized and then referred to in the main body; otherwise, it has no business being in your paper.

You can do it too! Outline your paper.

To recap and see how much you remember, try this little writing exercise! Don't be afraid to revisit the Train to make sure you include important points for each section when writing.

_____

_____

_____

_____

_____

_____

_____

_____

_____

_____

WHICH SECTION SHOULD I START WITH?

Although there isn't a rigid *"you should do this first and that second!"* type of formula, most people suggest starting with your methods, then moving on to results, discussion, introduction and literature review, conclusion, abstract, and finally, the title.

This is a logical way, because you can write the methods while you are planning and structuring it. Once you have your results, write and discuss them! You can write the introduction and literature review now because you probably have already collected articles and understand the background context better. With all of the main body sections, you can conclude and write an abstract to sum it all up. A lot of people suggest writing the title last because it gives you time throughout the research to think about it and, once everything is almost set in stone, you know what title would best represent your study.

This is just a suggestion, and no one is stopping you from writing everything in chronological order and following the Train. That makes sense too, because you are starting with what the literature has said about your topic and getting the background knowledge first before tackling the data, experiments, and whatnot.

~ CHAPTER SUMMARY ~

★ Research output usually takes the form of a book, journal article, or report.

★ Keep your audience in mind when determining your writing style.

★ Think about how you can let your story shine through in the paper.

★ A paper's typical structure is: title page, abstract, introduction, literature review, methodology, findings, discussion, conclusion, acknowledgments, references, and appendices. Not all sections have to be included.

★ The title is the first impression and should be succinct, specific, and symbolic (the three S's) of your research.

★ An abstract is your research paper in a nutshell (basically a paragraph summarizing the entire thing).

★ An introduction should be attention-grabbing, address why people should care about the topic, and introduce your paper's rationale, methods, and structure.

★ A literature review covers the important papers that inspired your paper or is prominent in the field. You can organize this chronologically, thematically, methodologically, or theoretically.

★ The methodology section should introduce your methods, establish why they are relevant, explain the tools you used to collect data and how you used them, and report how you analyzed the results.

★ The findings section presents your data and collected information in a digestible way for readers, such as using tables, graphs, charts, explanations in sentence form, etc.

★ The discussion is where findings are interpreted. It's where you reflect and discuss the significance of your new insights.

★ The conclusion is a summary of the main points and where future research suggestions are made. It is also where you admit your research's limitations.

★ Acknowledgments are an opportunity to give thanks to those who helped you along the way.

★ References are where you give credit to existing research that you built on in your paper. These should follow a consistent style.

★ An appendix, often optional, is the part where information that was too detailed or long to be in the paper's main body can be put.

★ There isn't a rigid schedule for which section to write first, but it can be helpful to write it like so: methodology, results, discussion, introduction and literature review, conclusion, abstract, and the title.

Chapter 10

Dressing Up before the Victory: Formatting References

"You can have anything you want in life if you dress for it."

–*Edith Head* (1887–1981), American costume designer

IT IS ALMOST TIME TO celebrate your work! Let's "dress to impress" the judges. After all, victory is sweetest when your paper looks good and the whole world gets to know how great it is. This is an accomplishment that will stay with you for the rest of your life.

In general, any reference style for a journal article will include authors' names and initials, the title of the article, the name of the journal, volume and issue, date, page numbers, and a Digital Object Identifier (DOI). DOIs are never-changing strings of numbers, letters, and symbols assigned to documents that are published online, but they aren't always applicable. Together, these parts are the essential pieces of a properly written reference—like the shirt, pants, socks, and shoes to your typical outfit.

MAJOR FORMATTING STYLES

Each journal is different and uses a different formatting style that you should adhere to. If you are writing a book, please note that every publisher might require various specific ways of formatting. If you are submitting to a conference or science/social science research competition, again, they will have their own formatting requirements.

There are a few major formatting styles used in academic texts:

- AMA (American Medical Association) for medicine, health, and biological sciences
- APA (American Psychological Association) for education, psychology, and the social sciences
- Chicago—a common style used in everyday publications like magazines, newspapers, and books

- MLA (Modern Language Association) for English, literature, arts, and humanities
- Turabian for its universal application across all subjects and disciplines

You can find the details for how to properly reference using each of these styles by searching up ⎯⎯⎯⎯⎯⎯⎯⎯⎯⎯⎯ style reference." Many libraries (online and offline) have complete guides that you can bookmark as great resources!

Here is an example of a basic in-text citation in APA Style: "Liu (2023) defined..." or "This is a fact (Liu, 2023)." You can see here that it's super simple!

Table 10.1 APA Style

Page Margins	1" on all sides (top, bottom, left, right)
Font	12-pt. Times Roman or Courier. For figures, however, use a sans-serif font such as Arial.
Spacing	Double-spaced

Alignment of Text	Flush left (with an uneven right margin)
Paragraph Indentation	5–7 spaces
End of Sentence	Leave one space after a period unless your teacher prefers two.
Page Numbers	On every page (except Figures), in the upper right margin, 1/2" from the top and flush with the right margin, two or three words of the paper title (this is called the running head) appear five spaces to the left of the page number, beginning with the title page.
Title Page	The title page is always the first page. On the line below the page number, the running head is typed flush left (all uppercase) following the words "Running head:". Below the running head, the following are centered on their own lines, using upper and lower case: • Paper title • Your name • Your school

Section Headings	Top-level headings should be centered on the page, using upper and lower case. Second-level headings should be flush left, italicized, using upper and lower case.
Tables & Illustrations	Unless your teacher tells you otherwise, tables and illustrations appear at the end of the paper. Each table begins on a separate page with the label Table 1 (etc.) typed flush left on the first line below the page number. Double-space and type the table title flush left (italicized using uppercase and lowercase letters). Figure captions appear on the last numbered page of the paper. In this case the label Figure 1 (etc.) is italicized and the caption itself is not. The caption uses regular sentence capitalization. The figures themselves follow, one per page.
Order of Major Sections	Each of these sections (if present) begins on a new page: • Title page • Abstract • Body • References • Appendixes

Source: APA Style, 2023, https://apastyle.apa.org/.

❤ **Little Nudge.** Take it easy; you don't have to purposefully memorize this! Just follow the style that your targeted journal prefers. Once you do research for a while and use a particular style a lot, you may end up subconsciously remembering anyway.

✷ **You can do it too!** Look in the mirror to double-check your "outfit": a checklist for after you completed the paper.

Does your paper...

- Follow a systematic and appropriate research methodology (Thattamparambil, 2020).

- Collect relevant data and use the right data-analysis methods.

- Builds on previous research.

- Use relevant, empirical data and proper data analysis.

- Represent a large population and can be generalized.

- Use logic to arrive at valid conclusions (Golesh et al., 2019).

- Enable others to replicate your experiment because your methodology is transparent.

- Acknowledge its limitations and provide suggestions for future research.

- Stay true to being ethical!

- Follow a consistent format throughout, especially in the references.

~ CHAPTER SUMMARY ~

★ Each research output has different formatting style requirements.

★ The major styles used in academic texts are AMA, APA, Chicago, MLA, and Turabian.

★ See the examples (APA Style) for specific requirements. Remember that online libraries are great tools for citing in a specific style.

LEVEL UP!

Chapter 11

Share Your Glory:
Dissemination

*"The goal of education is the advancement of
knowledge and the dissemination of truth."-*

–JOHN F. KENNEDY (1917–1963), 35th president of the United States

CONGRATULATIONS! IF YOU HAVE MADE it to this step, you have
worked incredibly hard; don't forget to be proud of yourself! Just
like in a video game where you can screenshot your results and
send them to a friend or post it online, now is the stage where
you make yourself known by sharing your paper.

WHAT IS DISSEMINATION?

Dissemination refers to "a planned process that involves consideration of target audiences and the settings in which research findings are to be received and, where appropriate, communicating and interacting with wider policy and…service audiences in ways that will facilitate research uptake in decision-making processes and practice" (Wilson et al., 2010, p. 91).

Put simply, this is a process that involves planning, thinking, considering your target audience, and communicating with that audience. This can be through journal publications, presentations, or popular media outlets and social media (to the general public).

JOURNAL PUBLICATION

Researchers commonly submit manuscripts to academic journals after completing a paper. These journals are usually read by other researchers, scholars, and practitioners, which is why it is called "peer-reviewed."

Peer review is a formal process in which other scholars review submitted work to ensure it is of high quality before publication. Because this is a rigorous process, publishing in a peer-reviewed journal is very prestigious and an achievement that will benefit you for your whole life!

A manuscript may be rejected by a journal after being submitted. Usually, even if a manuscript is accepted for publication, the peer reviewers will request improvements and changes to it before it can be published. This process helps improve the quality of journal articles and research.

Maybe all of this talk about sharing your work has made you a bit skeptical. "Why should I share *my precious* paper? Won't people laugh at me for trying to publicize my work?"

WHY RISK HARSH CRITICISM?

While I understand that you would want to safeguard your work from the harsh, outside world, people in academia won't laugh at you for publishing something. In fact, they will usually honor it because publishing is no easy feat.

♥ **Little Nudge.** Try to look from a different perspective. If people start looking for all the reasons why your paper is "bad" and their reasons are genuinely valid and reasonable, it's constructive criticism. This can be extremely valuable because it's a chance *for you to improve yourself.*

If an anonymous reviewer gives you a ton of comments and you are in despair because it looks like you need to rewrite the paper (and you might be angry too—why would they be so mean?), wait. Revisit the comments later. Think of it this way: the reviewer, someone who doesn't know you, is spending their time to make sure your paper is good. If they didn't care, it would've made their life a lot easier to simply reject the paper with no justification.

This is an opportunity for you to correct possible problems with your manuscript or find a journal that is a better fit for your research findings.

PRESENTATIONS

Getting your work published in a journal is challenging and time-consuming as journals receive many submissions but have limited room to publish. This is why another strategy is...*drum-roll, please*...presentations!

These can help you in the publication process since they are more accessible and provide more opportunities to share research while adhering to stringent standards. You can do this by submitting your work to conferences, workshops, or professional meetings as excellent ways to get feedback that isn't too harsh yet.

HOW TO EVALUATE YOUR EFFORTS?

Evaluating and reflecting on your efforts is essential because you can realize what worked for you and what didn't. This process is personalized and it's up to you to figure out what you would avoid during your next papers.

 You can do it too! Assessing your research activities.

Quantitative indicators:

- How much time and effort were spent
- Citations of your publications
- Numbers of events held for specific audiences
- Numbers of participants
- Amount of production and circulation of printed materials
- Metrics related to websites and social media platforms such as updates, visits, interactions, likes, and reposts. (Please don't go crazy over this one though, because "likes" on social media are often out of your control and do not determine the success of your research.)
- Media coverage such as articles in specialized press newsletters, press releases, interviews, and so on.

Qualitative indicators:

- How you felt in terms of energy level after each activity (energized, tired but happy, or burnt out?)
- Newly established contacts with networks and partners and the outcomes of these contacts
- Feedback from your target audience

HINT. You may want to keep a general estimate or log of how much time you spend, because it'll help you find more efficient ways of achieving the same results.

~ *CHAPTER SUMMARY* ~

★ Dissemination is a process that involves planning, thinking, considering your target audience, and communicating with that audience.

★ Peer-reviewed journal publication is a rigorous and difficult process that ensures high-quality publications. This is why achieving this is so beneficial.

★ Don't be afraid of criticism; embrace it as a chance to improve yourself and your paper.

★ Presenting your research at a conference, workshop, or meeting is another way to disseminate but is less "harsh" than submitting to a journal.

★ Reflect on and evaluate your research activities to find what fits you.

Chapter 12
Unlocking a Massive Treasure Chest of Useful Opportunities (Part I): Programs

"One opportunity leads directly to another."

—MARK US ZUSAK (1975-), Australian writer and author of
The Book Thief and *The Messenger*

THERE ARE A LOT of exciting opportunities that will help you learn subject-specific knowledge and skills and build a network with professionals in your interested research field. Many expose you to experiences working with professors—take this as a chance to learn about their research and see if you can help them! If you can build a strong working relationship with professors, you can ask them for letters of recommendation for these programs or to mentor you personally.

Below is a massive list of programs available for you to participate in based on disciplines (areas of study) ranging from the arts, language, and journalism to economics and STEM. The STEM section might be something you want to reference, especially if you want to do scientific lab research.

Please remember that no one in their right mind expects you to do every program offered (not even within a discipline!). It is up to you to evaluate which ones are the best fit for you, especially considering each program's location. The brief descriptions are based on the ones that the programs provide on their websites, so be sure to explore them on your own for details. Or, if this is a bit overwhelming right now, feel free to revisit this on your own time.

Besides these programs being ways to launch your research career by working with professors and professionals, having initial research experience plays an important role in your application during these programs. It's a promising indicator that you are capable of greatness. Who wouldn't want that? Also, a lot of these are challenging programs that may be easier to handle if you have research experience.

�֎ **You can do it too!** Highlighting some programs.

On the digital notebook file (see the QR code on page 32), you can access a complete list of all these programs. It might be easier to go through that so you don't have to manually enter the website links. Work with this in the way that works best for you, though.

Happy exploring and good luck!

ART, MUSIC, DANCE, AND THEATER

Art Summer Institute

- **Where?** California, USA. Has a virtual option.
- **What?** Two weeks of studio work, artist lectures, group critiques, and one-on-one meetings with faculty.
- **Who?** 8th–12th graders.
https://summer.ucla.edu/program/art-summer-institute/

Aspire: Five-Week Music Performance Intensive

- **Where?** Berklee College of Music, Massachusetts, USA.
- **What?** Five weeks in the summer of one-on-one instruction to enhance instrumental or vocal performance, weekly private lessons, and elective coursework.
- **Who?** Ages 15+ with six months of playing or singing experience.
https://www.berklee.edu/summer/programs/five-week

Blue Lake Fine Arts Camp

- **Where?** Michigan, USA.

- **What?** Summer school with programs in music, art, dance, and drama.

- **Who?** Elementary, junior high, and high school students.
https://bluelake.org/

Chautauqua Institution

- **Where?** New York, USA.

- **What?** Summer classes in art, theater, music, and dance that bring talented artists from worldwide to their grounds.

- **Who?** Check the specific programs.
https://www.chq.org/festival-schools/

Interlochen Summer Arts Camp

- **Where?** Michigan, USA.

- **What?** Many summer camp programs in creative writing, dance, film and new media, interdisciplinary arts, music, theater, and visual arts.

- **Who?** Multiple age ranges (grades 3–12) depending on the program.

http://camp.interlochen.org/

MICA PreCollege

- **Where?** Maryland Institute College of Art (MICA), Maryland, USA.

- **What?** Summer pre-college on campus with college-level art and design experiences to earn up to three college credits.

- **Who?** Rising high school junior and senior artists and designers.
https://www.mica.edu/non-degree-learning-oppor-tunities/programs-for-youth/programs-for-teens/summer-pre-college-program

Parsons Intensives and Summer Program

- **Where?** Parsons School of Design, New York, USA. Has a virtual option.

- **What?** Summer programs to learn skills, develop portfolios, earn college credits, and explore creative professions.

- **Who?** All ages (grade 3 to working professionals).
https://www.newschool.edu/parsons/summer-programs

Pratt Pre-College

- **Where?** Pratt Institute, New York, USA.

- **What?** College-level summer or spring/fall program to earn college credits in art, design, architecture, or creative writing from courses taught by Pratt Institute's faculty.

- **Who?** High school students.
https://www.pratt.edu/continuing-and-professional-studies/precollege/

SCAD Pre-College Program

- **Where?** Savannah College of Art and Design, multiple locations in Georgia, USA.

- **What?** Summer and throughout the year pre-college programs with opportunities for art and design while working with peers.

- **Who?** High school students.
https://www.scad.edu/academics/pre-college-programs

RISD Pre-Collegiate Program

- **Where?** Rhode Island School of Design, Rhosde Island, USA. Has a virtual year-long option.

- **What?** Five-week college-level curriculum with studio classes, critiques, and projects to experience life as a RISD undergraduate student.

- **Who?** Rising high school juniors and seniors.
https://precollege.risd.edu

Summer Programs at Juilliard

- **Where?** The Juilliard School, New York, USA.

- **What?** Summer programs for artists at any skill level.

- **Who?** Check the specific programs.
https://www.juilliard.edu/juilliard-all/summer-programs

The California State Summer School for the Arts

- **Where?** California, USA.

- **What?** Multiple programs in the visual and performing arts, creative writing, animation, and film.

- **Who?** High-school-aged artists.
https://www.csssa.ca.gov/

The Culture, Design and Fine Arts in New York (CDFNY) Summer Program

- **Where?** School of Visual Arts, New York City, USA.
- **What?** Summer program to experience NYC while developing creative abilities.
- **Who?** International college students. https://sva.edu/academics/study-abroad/summer-program-in-nyc

The Met High School Internship Program

- **Where?** The Metropolitan Museum of Art, New York, USA.
- **What?** Paid summer internship to connect with art, museums, and creative professionals as well as gain work experience.
- **Who?** Grades 10–11 in New York, New Jersey, or Connecticut. https://www.metmuseum.org/about-the-met/internships/high-school/summer-high-school-internships

Tisch High School Programs

- **Where?** New York University Tisch School of the Arts, New York, USA. Has a virtual option.
- **What?** Various programs are taught by NYU faculty to provide a college experience and develop a career in the arts.
- **Who?** High school students.

http://tisch.nyu.edu/special-programs/high-school-programs

University of Southern California School of Cinematic Arts

- **Where?** California, USA.
- **What?** Learning disciplines for entering the entertainment industry in the future.
- **Who?** Check the specific programs.
https://cinema.usc.edu/programs/index.cfm

Visual Arts Summer Institute

- **Where?** Boston University College of Fine Arts, Massachusetts, USA.
- **What?** Summer visual arts program to build exceptional portfolios and experience college art school.
- **Who?** High school students (ages 15–18).
http://www.bu.edu/cfa/vasi/

BUSINESS AND ECONOMICS

Berkeley Business Academy for Youth

- **Where?** Haas School of Business at the University of California, Berkeley, California, USA.

- **What?** Two-week spring or summer program teaching business skills for a college life experience.

- **Who?** Middle and high school students (check the specific programs).
  https://haas.berkeley.edu/business-academy/

LaunchX High School Entrepreneurship Summer Program

- **Where?** Multiple locations depending on the program. Has a virtual option.

- **What?** Entrepreneurship summer program that brings resources, skills, the mindset, and networks to students for launching a successful business.

- **Who?** High school students.
  https://launchx.com/

Leadership in the Business World (LBW)

- **Where?** Wharton Global Youth Program through the Wharton School of the University of Pennsylvania, Pennsylvania, USA.

- **What?** Summer program to introduce undergraduate business, leadership, teamwork, and communication education.

- **Who?** Rising senior high school students.
  https://globalyouth.wharton.upenn.edu/programs-courses/
  leadership-in-the-business-world/

Management & Technology Summer Institute

- **Where?** Jerome Fisher Program in Management & Technology at the Wharton School of the University of Pennsylvania, Pennsylvania, USA.
- **What?** A three-week summer program with college credits taught by UPenn faculty and entrepreneurs to link technology and management concepts.
- **Who?** Rising high school seniors and juniors.

https://fisher.wharton.upenn.edu/management-technology-summer-institute/

Moneyball Academy

- **Where?** Wharton Global Youth Program through the Wharton School of the University of Pennsylvania, Pennsylvania, USA.
- **What?** A three-week summer program for studying sports analytics.
- **Who?** Rising high school seniors and juniors.

https://globalyouth.wharton.upenn.edu/programs-courses/moneyball-academy/

The Kelley Women's Leadership Institute

- **Where?** Kelley School of Business at Indiana University, Indiana, USA.
- **What?** A week at Indiana University for a college experience and exploration of business career opportunities.
- **Who?** Young women. Check the specific program dates for age range.

https://kelley.iu.edu/programs/undergrad/pre-college/ywi.html

FOREIGN LANGUAGE, HISTORY, AND HUMANITIES

The Concord Review History Camp

- **Where?** Massachusetts, USA. Has a virtual option.

- **What?** A workshop in historical research where students write a first draft of a paper on their chosen topic.

- **Who?** High school and middle school students.
  https://www.varsityacademics.org/history-camp-overview

National Security Language Initiative for Youth (NSLI-Y)

- **Where?** In places where Arabic, Chinese (Mandarin), Hindi, Indonesian, Korean, Persian (Tajiki), Russian, or Turkish are spoken through the US Department of State.

- **What?** Scholarships for participating in overseas language study programs during the summer and academic year.

- **Who?** US high school students.
  https://exchanges.state.gov/us/program/nsliy

Stanford Summer Humanities Institute

- **Where?** Stanford University, California, USA.
- **What?** A three-week summer program where students explore questions at the heart of humanities led by Stanford professors.
- **Who?** Rising high school juniors and seniors.
https://summerhumanities.spcs.stanford.edu/

JOURNALISM

The California Scholastic Press Association

- **Where?** California, USA.
- **What?** A twelve-day program for building networks with professional journalists and developing necessary skills.
- **Who?** High school students.
https://cspaworkshop.org/

The Princeton Summer Journalism Program

- **Where?** Princeton University, New Jersey, USA.

- **What?** Year-long college-prep program with workshops and lectures by renowned journalists.

- **Who?** High school juniors.
https://psjp.princeton.edu/

Summer Academy

- **Where?** The School of The New York Times, New York, USA.

- **What?** Understanding the world through learning experiences led by New York Times experts.

- **Who?** Grades 10–12, age 15+.
https://nytedu.com/admissions/

SCIENCE, TECHNOLOGY, ENGINEERING, AND MATH (STEM)

1000 Girls 1000 Futures

- **Where?** Online through the New York Academy of Sciences.

- **What?** A groundbreaking program engaging young women in STEM through mentoring and twenty-first-century skills development.

- **Who?** Young women ages 13–17 from around the world. https://www.nyas.org/programs/global-stem-alliance/ 1000-girls-1000-futures/

Art of Problem Solving

- **Where?** Online.

- **What?** Interactive online math courses that run all year long, led by experts in advanced math.

- **Who?** Grades 5–12. https://artofproblemsolving.com/

Boston Leadership Institute

- **Where?** Massachusetts, USA.

- **What?** Three-week or one-week summer programs in STEM classes and advanced research.

- **Who?** High school students. https://www.bostonleadershipinstitute.com/

California State Summer School for Mathematics & Science (COSMOS)

- **Where?** California, USA.

- **What?** A four-week summer program where students work with renowned faculty, researchers, and scientists to explore advanced STEM topics.

- **Who?** California students in grades 8–12. https://cosmos-ucop.ucdavis.edu

Clemson and PARI Space Exploration Camps

- **Where?** Clemson University, South Carolina, USA.

- **What?** A summer research program where students use NASA-built radio telescopes and other advanced tools to conduct research while mentored by astronomers and scientists.

- **Who?** Middle and high school students.

https://scienceweb.clemson.edu/cusoc/clemson-space-camps/

CATALYST Academy

- **Where?** Cornell Engineering at Cornell University, New York, USA.

- **What?** A one-week engineering program on-campus for an authentic college experience.

- **Who?** High school juniors and seniors attending high school in the USA.

https://sites.coecis.cornell.edu/catalystacademy/

Girls Who Code Summer Programs

- **Where?** Online.

- **What?** Free summer programs (live or self-paced) to gain computer science skills and prepare for tech careers.

- **Who?** 9th–11th graders that identify as girls or non-binary.

https://girlswhocode.com/programs/summer-immersion-program

High School Honors Science/Engineering/Mathematics Program (HSHSP)

- **Where?** Michigan State University, Michigan, USA.

- **What?** A seven-week, on-campus summer research program to conduct research.

- **Who?** 11th grade students who are US citizens and permanent residents.
  https://education.msu.edu/hshsp/

Johns Hopkins Engineering Innovation Pre-College Programs

- **Where?** Johns Hopkins Whiting School of Engineering, Maryland, USA. Has a virtual option.

- **What?** A college-level summer program for students interested in math, science, and engineering.

- **Who?** High school students.
  https://ei.jhu.edu/

Kode With Klossy Summer Camps

- **Where?** Online and many in-person locations.

- **What?** A free, two-week summer camp that introduces computer science concepts and skills for students to explore the possibilities of technology.

- **Who?** Those who identify as women, gender nonconforming, or trans, ages 13–18.
  https://www.kodewithklossy.com/

LIVE by Po Shen Loh

- **Where?** Online.

- **What?** Inspiring math classes that cover competition-level math and tools for innovation using interactive tools.

- **Who?** Anyone, any grade level, from anywhere!
https://live.poshenloh.com/

Michigan Math and Science Scholars

- **Where?** University of Michigan College of Literature, Science, and the Arts, Michigan, USA.

- **What?** A two-week program to expose students to a pre-college experience for scientific research.

- **Who?** High school rising sophomores, juniors, or seniors from around the world.
https://sites.lsa.umich.edu/mmss/

MIT PRIMES

- **Where?** Massachusetts Institute of Technology, Massachusetts, USA.

- **What?** A free, year-long after-school program where students work with MIT researchers on problems in math, computer science, and computational biology.

- **Who?** High school students within driving distance from Boston.
https://math.mit.edu/research/highschool/primes/program

MITES

- **Where?** Massachusetts Institute of Technology, Massachusetts, USA.

- **What?** Free programs for students to build foundations in STEM and increase confidence.
- **Who?** 7th–12th grade students.

https://mites.mit.edu/

PREFACE: The Rensselaer Summer Engineering Design Program

- **Where?** Rensselaer Polytechnic Institute, New York, USA.
- **What?** A fourteen-day program to have a college experience in science, engineering, and other technological fields.
- **Who?** 11th and 12th grade students.

https://info.rpi.edu/pre-college-initiatives/preface-2022-rensselaer-summer-engineering-design-program

PRIMES-USA

- **Where?** Online.
- **What?** A free, year-long mathematical research program where students work on projects under the mentorship of graduate students and faculty from MIT and other universities.
- **Who?** High school sophomores and juniors from the USA.

https://math.mit.edu/research/highschool/primes/usa/

Research Scholar Program for High School Students

- **Where?** Garcia Center at Stony Brook University, New York, USA.

- **What?** A seven-week program with formal instruction and independent research programs under guidance from Garcia Center faculty.

- **Who?** High school students.
https://www.stonybrook.edu/commcms/garcia/summer_program/program_description.php

Research Internships in Science & Engineering (RISE)

- **Where?** Boston University, Massachusetts, USA.

- **What?** A six-week program to conduct lab research while advancing STEM knowledge.

- **Who?** High school juniors.
https://www.bu.edu/mysummer/academics/research-internship-in-science-engineering/

Research Science Institute (RSI)

- **Where?** Massachusetts Institute of Technology, Massachusetts, USA.

- **What?** A free summer program where students research scientific theories in science, engineering, and technology.

- **Who?** One hundred of the world's most accomplished high school students.
https://www.cee.org/programs/research-science-institute

Roswell Park Cancer Institute K–12 and Undergrad Programs

- **Where?** New York, USA.

- **What?** A summer program for researching at America's Cancer Research Center.

- **Who?** Check the specific programs.
https://www.roswellpark.org/education/summer-programs

Sea Camp Residential Camp

- **Where?** Texas A&M University at Galveston, Texas, USA.

- **What?** A week-long where students explore marine wonders and access research vessels, equipment, lab facilities, and professional staff.

- **Who?** Ages 10–18.
https://www.tamug.edu/seacamp

Secondary Student Training Program

- **Where?** Belin-Blank Center at the University of Iowa, Iowa, USA.

- **What?** Program where students research under the mentorship of world-class faculty and realize their academic goals.

- **Who?** Grades 10–11.
https://belinblank.education.uiowa.edu/students/sstp/

Summer Engineering Institute (SEI)

- **Where?** Lehigh University, Pennsylvania, USA.

- **What?** A four-week summer program on campus where students research intensively and enhance their engineering and technological skills.

- **Who?** Rising high school juniors and seniors.
https://engineering.lehigh.edu/about/engineering-outreach/sei

Stanford Artificial Intelligence Laboratory's Outreach Summer Program (SAILORS)

- **Where?** Online.

- **What?** A three-week program to train students to become AI researchers and increase diversity in computer science.

- **Who?** 9th grade students.
https://ai.stanford.edu/outreach/

Stanford Medical Youth Science Program

- **Where?** Online.

- **What?** A free, five-week program on science and medicine.

- **Who?** High school juniors who live in Northern and Central California.
https://smysp.spcs.stanford.edu/

Students and Teachers As Research Scientists (STARS)

- **Where?** University of Missouri–St. Louis, Missouri, USA.

- **What?** A summer program that introduces aspects of the scientific enterprise.

- **Who?** Rising high school juniors and seniors.
https://www.umsl.edu/~sep/STARS/index.html

Summer Immersion: New York City

- **Where?** Columbia University, New York, USA.

- **What?** Various pre-college courses to challenge and engage students while allowing them to experience college life.

- **Who?** Students in grades 9–12 or freshman year of college from around the world.
https://precollege.sps.columbia.edu/highschool/summer-immersion-new-york-city

Summer Program on Applied Rationality and Cognition (SPARC)

- **Where?** California, USA.

- **What?** A free summer program to develop quantitative skills with undergraduate- and graduate-level concepts and apply them to the world.

- **Who?** High school students and first-year undergraduates.
https://sparc-camp.org/

The Anson L. Clark Scholar Program

- **Where?** Texas Tech University, USA.

- **What?** A free, seven-week summer research program with practical research experiences.

- **Who?** Twelve high school juniors and seniors (age 17+)
https://www.depts.ttu.edu/honors/academicsand
enrichment/affiliatedandhighschool/clarks/

The Engineering Summer Academy at Penn (ESAP)

- **Where?** University of Pennsylvania School of Engineering and Applied Science, Pennsylvania, USA.

- **What?** A three-week program to explore college-level engineering with hands-on experience in technologies.

- **Who?** High school students.
https://esap.seas.upenn.edu/

The International Summer School for Young Physicists (ISSYP)

- **Where?** Online.
- **What?** A two-week summer program focusing on theoretical physics and physics studies.
- **Who?** Canadian and international high school students. https://apply.perimeterinstitute.ca/prog/_2023_issyp/

The Junior Academy

- **Where?** Online.
- **What?** A year-long program with ten-week challenge periods where students work together on international teams with a STEM professional mentor to compete in research project-based challenges with a focus on the United Nations Sustainable Development Goals.
- **Who?** Students aged 13–17 from around the world. https://www.nyas.org/programs/global-stem-alliance/the-junior-academy/

The National High School Game Academy (NHSGA)

- **Where?** Carnegie Mellon University, Pennsylvania, USA.
- **What?** A six-week program where you develop video games using current industry best practices.
- **Who?** High school students aged 16+. https://www.cmu.edu/pre-college/academic-programs/game-academy.html

The Simons Summer Research Program

- **Where?** SUNY Stony Brook University, New York, USA.

- **What?** A summer program to undertake hands-on research in a variety of disciplines, ranging from science and math to engineering.

- **Who?** High school students aged 16+.
https://www.stonybrook.edu/simons/

The Stanford Institutes of Medicine Summer Research Program (SIMR)

- **Where?** Stanford University, California, USA.

- **What?** An eight-week program to perform basic research with Stanford faculty, postdoctoral fellows, students, and researchers on a medically oriented project.

- **Who?** High school juniors and seniors (age 16+) who are permanent residents in the US.
https://simr.stanford.edu/

The Summer Science Program

- **Where?** Multiple locations.

- **What?** A residential enrichment program to complete a challenging, hands-on research project in astrophysics, biochemistry, or genomics.

- **Who?** 10th and 11th grade high school students.
https://summerscience.org/

The UCLA Nanoscience Lab Summer Institute

- **Where?** University of California, California, USA.

- **What?** A five-day summer workshop for those who are interested in advanced science and technology.

- **Who?** High school students with a background in chemistry.

http://summer.ucla.edu/institutes/NanoScienceLab

The Yale Summer Program in Astrophysics (YSPA)

- **Where?** Yale University, Connecticut, USA.

- **What?** A two-week online and four-week residential research and enrichment program in astronomy, physics, math, computer programming, and other science and tech fields.

- **Who?** Thirty-six rising seniors.

https://yspa.yale.edu/

The Young Scientist Program (YSP)

- **Where?** Washington University School of Medicine in St. Louis, Missouri, USA.

- **What?** Activities emphasizing hands-on research and individualized contact between young people and active scientists for the pursuit of STEM careers.

- **Who?** High school students from disadvantaged backgrounds.

https://sites.wustl.edu/wustlysp/

THINK

- **Where?** Massachusetts Institute of Technology, Massachusetts, USA.

- **What?** A science, research, and innovation program where students who have done background research on a potential research project are given guidance. Finalists are given up to $1,000 in funding and have weekly mentorship meetings with THINK team members.

- **Who?** High school students living in the United States.
https://think.mit.edu/

UC Davis Young Scholars Program

- **Where?** University of California, Davis, California, USA.

- **What?** A summer residential research program exposing students' original research in biology, agriculture, environment, and natural sciences.

- **Who?** Forty high school students (rising juniors or rising seniors).
https://ysprogram.ucdavis.edu/

Research Mentorship Program

- **Where?** University of California, Santa Barbara, California, USA.

- **What?** A competitive summer program to experience interdisciplinary, hands-on, university-level research. Students have a mentor and choose a research project.

- **Who?** High school students from all over the world.
https://www.summer.ucsb.edu/pre-college/research-mentorship-program/application-and-fees

OTHER

Girls Leadership Academy Meetup Events and Ambassador Program

- **Where?** California, USA, or online.

- **What?** Free events to empower girls with leadership, public speaking, coding, business planning, creativity, teamwork, entrepreneurship, and strategic skills through inspirational speakers and a carefully designed curriculum.

- **Who?** Girls aged 8–12.
https://www.glam-readytolead.com/

Khan Academy

- **Where?** Online.

- **What?** Free online courses with lessons covering K–12 math, grammar, science, history, AP®, SAT®, and more to provide world-class education.

- **Who?** Anyone, any grade level, from anywhere!
https://www.khanacademy.org/

Perry Research Scholars Institute (PRSI)

- **Where?** Belin-Blank Center at the University of Iowa, Iowa, USA.

- **What?** A two-week, residential summer program where students participate in seminars with university faculty and are introduced to research in fields such as anthropology, business, education, engineering, medicine, psychology, sustainability, etc.

- **Who?** High school students.

https://belinblank.education.uiowa.edu/students/prsi/

Secondary Student Training Program (Iowa)

- **Where?** Belin-Blank Center at the University of Iowa, Iowa, USA.

- **What?** A five-week research program to guide students to complete university-level research by working with a faculty mentor.

- **Who?** High school students.

https://belinblank.education.uiowa.edu/students/sstp/

UConn Mentor Connection

- **Where?** University of Connecticut, Connecticut, USA.

- **What?** To provide students with opportunities to participate in creative projects and investigations under the supervision of university mentors.

- **Who?** Rising high school juniors and seniors.

https://achieve.uconn.edu/connects/

YOUNGA

- **Where?** Online.

- **What?** A four-week leadership training program to not only listen to live sessions with world leaders and influencers but also be a part of the largest global festival for impacting the world.

- **Who?** Young leaders under the age of thirty from around the world.

https://youngaworld.com/

Chapter 13

Unlocking a Massive Treasure Chest of Useful Opportunities (Part II): Competitions, Scholarships, and Funding

"It's good to have high-quality competition; it helps drive research forward at a faster pace."

–Shuji Nakamura (1954–), Japanese-born American engineer and inventor

ENTERING A RESEARCH COMPETITION DEMONSTRATES that you have great passion for your research field, take initiative, show commitment, and care about academics beyond the grades in your courses. Participation in competitions is a strong extracurricular activity, and successes—like making the finals or winning—can provide you with chances to earn scholarships. This can even open doors for other opportunities, such as public speaking, internships, and part-time jobs.

No matter if you win or lose, it gives you opportunities to reflect on what you have learned and improve yourself. Here is a list of research competitions for your consideration.

🌟 **You can do it too!** Highlight some competitions, scholarships, or funding.

Just like the previous chapter, the digital notebook file has all of the following links and what the opportunity is called.

Breakthrough Junior Challenge

- **What?** A global competition to inspire creative scientific thinking by having students submit original videos for a $250,000 scholarship, a $50,000 teacher prize, and a $100,000 school science lab.

- **Who?** Students aged 13 to 18.
  https://breakthroughjuniorchallenge.org/

China Thinks Big (CTB)

- **What?** A high school research and innovation competition tackling important issues posed by professors at Harvard and other top institutions.

- **Who?** High school students in China.
https://www.hauscr.org/ctb

Davidson Fellows Scholarship

- **What?** A prestigious scholarship ($50,000, $25,000, and $10,000) to high-achieving students given by Davidson Institute.

- **Who?** Only US students 18 years old or under who have completed a significant piece of work/study in STEM, literature, music, philosophy, or something outside-the-box. Only open to US citizens residing in or permanent residents of the United States.
https://www.davidsongifted.org/gifted-programs/fellows-scholarship/

Future Business Leaders of America, Inc. (FBLA) Competitions

- **What?** FBLA hosts challenges each year to leverage design thinking to develop innovative solutions that help increase access to entrepreneurship and small-business ownership for underrepresented groups. Winning teams will receive $5,000, $3,000, $2,000, and/or $250 in prizes.

- **Who?** High school students around the world.
https://www.fbla.org/divisions/pbl/pbl-competitive-events/

Global Essay Competition

- **What?** Essay competition in seven subjects: philosophy, politics, economics, history, psychology, theology, and law hosted by the John Locke Institute.

- **Who?** Students aged 18 or younger around the world. https://www.johnlockeinstitute.com/essay-competition

Harvard International Economics Essay Contest (HIEEC)

- **What?** Economic essay contest. The top three winning essays will be published in the Harvard Economics Review online publications.

- **Who?** High school students around the world. https://www.thehuea.org/hieec

The Diamond Challenge

- **What?** A global, high school entrepreneurship competition offering $100,000 in prizes and resources to take student ideas to the next level.

- **Who?** For any teen from any location with any idea. https://diamondchallenge.org/

The *Harvard International Review* Academic Writing Contest

- **What?** Academic writing contest on topics related to international affairs.

- **Who?** High school students around the world. https://hir.harvard.edu/contest/

iGEM

- **What?** An annual, worldwide synthetic biology event. Multidisciplinary teams work together to design, build, and test a system of their own using interchangeable biological parts and standard molecular biology techniques.

- **Who?** High school, undergraduate, and graduate students.
https://competition.igem.org/

ISSCY

- **What?** Cohosted and sponsored by the World Federation of United Nations Associations (WFUNA) and GATSVI Challenge, ISSCY is an opportunity to submit a research proposal to promote the study of humanities and social science, and, if selected, submit a full paper. More than eighty young researchers may be given the opportunity to publish their work in ISSCY's online journal.

- **Who?** High school students around the world.
https://isscy.com

Junior Science and Humanities Symposium (JSHS)

- **What?** A STEM competition in research where students present their findings and compete for scholarships, aid, and opportunities.

- **Who?** High school students. Only open to US citizens residing in or permanent residents of the United States.
https://jshs.org/students/program-benefits/

Journal of Young Explorers Meta (JYEM) Competition

- **What?** Submit scholarly manuscripts or projects with various methods or in interdisciplinary fields to receive up to $1,000 in Amazon gift cards.

- **Who?** Grades 9–12 students around the world.
https://jyem.org/schedule.php

National History Day (NHD)

- **What?** A year-long academic program focused on historical research, interpretation, and creative expression.

- **Who?** All students grades 6–12.
https://www.nhd.org/why-nhd-works

Regeneron International Science and Engineering Fair

- **What?** The world's largest international, pre-college science competition to showcase students' independent research in a competition for $4 million in prizes.

- **Who?** High school students around the world.
https://www.societyforscience.org/isef/

Regeneron Science Talent Search (STS)

- **What?** It is considered the most prestigious high school science research competition in the nation. Competitors submit a completed independent research project to win up to $250,000.

- **Who?** High school seniors who are US citizens (even those who live abroad).
https://www.societyforscience.org/regeneron-sts/

The Conrad Challenge

- **What?** A purpose-driven innovation competition creating the next generation of entrepreneurs who will change the world by applying science, technology, and innovation to solve problems with global impact.
- **Who?** Students between the ages of 13–18 around the world.

https://www.conradchallenge.org/

The Marshall Society Essay Competition

- **What?** Economic essay contest hosted by the economics society at the University of Cambridge.
- **Who?** High school students around the world.

https://marshallsociety.com/essay-competition/

The Modeling the Future Challenge

- **What?** A real-world competition to conduct research modeling real-world data to analyze risks and make recommendations to companies, industry groups, governments, or organizations.
- **Who?** High school students around the world.

https://www.mtfchallenge.org/about/

The Clean Tech Competition

- **What?** It challenges students to make a significant environmental impact through designing innovative business plans with clean technology ideas. The winning entry receives an estimated prize of $25,000.

- **Who?** University students across the globe.
https://thecleantechchallenge.uk/

U.S. Stockholm Junior Water Prize

- **What?** A competition to develop research projects that can help solve major water challenges.

- **Who?** Students aged 15 to 20 around the world.
https://www.wef.org/membership--community/
students--young-professionals/sjwp/

Chapter 14

Becoming Diamond-Tier: Publication for Young Researchers

"This is the most beautiful thing we'll ever have to publish.
Let us print it if it's the last effort of our lives!"

—Margaret Caroline Anderson (1886–1973),
American founder, editor, and publisher of the art
and literary magazine The Little Review

WHY IS PUBLISHING IN A journal "diamond-tier," you may ask? This is one of the best and ultimate ways to acknowledge your work. Doing research alone is rare and impressive in academics, just like diamonds. If you can publish that research, it adds a layer of external legitimacy where your contribution to research is officially recognized.

Please note there are different channels through which to get your research published, with different levels of rigor and difficulty.

DIFFERENT TYPES OF PUBLICATION CHANNELS

Peer-reviewed publications: This is a rigorous process that can take a long time (even years!) where your paper is analyzed and critiqued before being ultimately accepted as legitimate. It's called "peer-reviewed" because fellow researchers in the same field will examine the paper and give feedback. This process is often double-blind, meaning that the reviewer does not know who the author is and the author does not know who the reviewer is.

HINT. Although this is difficult, it pays off! Publishing in a peer-reviewed journal is like acquiring the shiniest diamond.

Practitioner publications: Magazines, journals, newspapers, online blogs, or social media could also be your potential channels to have papers published. For example, there are online magazines like *Forbes* or the *Financial Times*, local newspapers, and online blogs like the *Huffington Post*.

HINT. This requires direct contact with an editorial manager, who can decide whether your work is appropriate or not. To get to these editorial managers, you'll need to do some online searching and send them an email with your pitch that explains why your work is relevant to their audience. Offering an "exclusive" can be one way to make it attractive to the editors.

Research conferences: An advantage of these is that they often accept abstracts of papers instead of the full text, making the amount of effort required to get accepted lower. You'll need to do some scouring to find the best-fit conferences for you.

Pay-to-play research journals (please *avoid* this!): There are some journals that will accept any paper as long as a fee is paid. Sound sketchy? That's right. These journals are academically unethical and can be a red flag in your credentials.

 You can do it too! Highlight some publication opportunities.

One last time—reference the digital notebook for all these links below!

ACADEMIC JOURNALS FOR YOUNG RESEARCHERS

$E=mc2$ is a math journal at the University of Chicago and is supported by the National Science Foundation.
https://mazziotti.uchicago.edu/journal/indyjo.html

Curieux Academic Journal is completely edited by high school students and accepts submissions on any serious topics.
https://www.curieuxacademicjournal.com/

International Journal of High School Research is a leading high school research journal. All manuscripts published are indexed internationally by EBSCO (a research database and platform), which makes them available to be searched by most libraries around the world. This selects high school research in all areas of science, including the behavioral and social sciences, technology, engineering, and math.
https://ijhighschoolresearch.org

Journal of Emerging Investigators is a science journal and mentorship program publishing research by middle and high school scientists.
https://emerginginvestigators.org/

Journal of High School Science is a peer-reviewed STEM Journal that publishes research and ideas from high school students.
https://jhss.scholasticahq.com/

Journal of Student Research is an academic, multidisciplinary, and faculty-reviewed journal based in Houston, Texas, devoted to publishing research by high school, undergraduate, and graduate students.
https://www.jsr.org/hs/index.php/path

Journal of Research High School is an international, open-access research journal exclusively for high school researchers. It invites original research and meaningful literature reviews in various fields of study such as engineering, humanities, natural science, mathematics, and social science.
https://www.journalresearchhs.org/about

Questioz is an international online journal of high school research in original work spanning all academic disciplines.
https://www.questioz.org/research

The Concord Review is the only quarterly journal in the world to publish academic research papers by secondary students, particularly in the historical field.
https://tcr.org/

The Columbia Junior Science Journal is a high school research journal for one- to two-page original research papers or two- to five-page review articles in the fields of natural sciences, physical sciences, engineering, and social sciences.
http://cjsjournal.org/

The National High School Journal of Science is a free, online, student-run, and peer-reviewed research journal that is targeted toward high school students. They accept original research, short articles, policy, technical comments, and letters.
https://nhsjs.com/?mainpage

The Schola is a quarterly journal of humanities and social sciences essays written by high school students around the world.
https://theschola.org

NON-ACADEMIC JOURNALS/MAGAZINES

Amazing Kids! is a monthly magazine that welcomes fiction and nonfiction.
https://amazing-kids.org/

Capulet Magazine is a literary magazine for young women to express their creativity in fiction, nonfiction, poetry, and art.
https://capuletmag.com/

Cathartic Youth Literary Magazine is an international online youth literary magazine on mental health and identity.
https://www.catharticlitmagazine.com/

Crashtest publishes poetry, stories, and creative nonfiction in the form of personal essays, imaginative inves-

tigation, and experimental interviews by high school teens in grades 9–12.
https://www.crashtestmag.com/

Ice Lolly Review is an online literary magazine for works with a "pastel theme" by young writers.
https://www.icelollyreview.com/

Teen Ink is a monthly tabloid-format magazine that is marketed to and written by teenagers. They accept many forms of media such as articles, poetry, art, photography, books, and videos.
http://www.teenink.com/

The Hoya provides a platform for young readers, writers, and artists aged 14–19 to express their "take on global issues to raise awareness and express their own stance on them."
https://thehoya.com/

The Ideate Review publishes fiction, poetry, and art related to identity from writers and artists aged 14+.
https://www.theideatereview.org/

The WEIGHT Journal is for high school students that creatively write about heavy topics. They accept all forms such as poetry, slam, flash fiction, short fiction, and more.
https://www.theweightjournal.com/

Conclusion

"No research without action, no action without research"

–*Kurt Lewin* (1890–1947), German-American social psychologist

FROM WHY YOU SHOULD RESEARCH, the rules of research, pitfalls to avoid, and choosing a topic to literature reviews, choosing a method, dealing with data, writing it up, and formatting references, you have learned quite a lot about how to do research. You're now also equipped with different paths you can take to disseminate what you have written, including unlocking a ton of resources to level up your research.

The goal of this book has been to inspire, support, and empower you, the next generation of aspiring young researchers in an engaging way. My goal has been to make research more fascinating and attractive. I hope what you can take away from this is that pursuing your personal research project can be empowering. Although there is no set step-by-step guide to do so, through this book, you know how to be motivated and find your own vibrant way of researching that is just like playing a game. Of course, I expect this book has demystified research to eliminate the assumption that it is something too complex and only for older people who are experts.

Once you have read this the first time, I hope you don't shove it in a dusty bookshelf and forget about it. Please use this as a resource and keep this within arm's length at your desk. Whenever you are in a slump or stuck in your research journey, open this up and be blasted with inspiration! I want you to think, "Since I see that this has been done before, I'm not crazy in thinking that I can do it too!"

During the process of doing research, you'll find a journey of exploration of questions, answers, truth, frustration, beauty, and all the ephemeral joys that create enduring memories. From my experience, I find it is important to focus on what is meaningful for me and what I am passionate about. This has helped me believe in myself, find my own ways, be courageous, never give up, and do great things. Again, you can do it too!

I also intended for this book to make the process of doing your own research simpler and more enjoyable. I hope that by now, using this book, you will have written at least one wonderful research paper or work to share with your peers, teachers, family, and the world!

The game isn't over, though; this is just the beginning. It's your turn to design your own path and become the person who makes others go, "Wow. They have achieved incredible things and they are just like me! *I can do it too.*"

Are you ready?

Best of luck!

Grace (signing out for now).

P.S. Contact me! I want to hear about how your research journey goes. Visit my website research2empower.org to shoot a message or email me directly at grace@research2empower. org. Since research is constantly evolving, if there are any inconsistencies or even invalid links in the treasure chest of resources, please email me (I greatly appreciate it)!

Also, keep an eye out for a free, colorful, and also incredibly vibrant research course as a supplement to this book on Research To Empower website https://www.research2empower.org/.

Acknowledgments

THIS BOOK INVOLVES FOUR YEARS of effort. A lot of people have helped me along the way with their time and selfless efforts, which I am forever thankful for. Firstly, I am deeply indebted to Dr. Willem Spanjers from the School of Economics, Kingston University, London. He constantly goes beyond the typical definition of a research mentor by teaching me not only how to do research but also to have a positive research mindset, which has been the best support and guidance I could've ever asked for. This book would not have been the same without his advice.

Secondly, I cannot express in words how much I love and appreciate my family for their constant encouragement, little daily motivating speeches, and for having faith in me and my crazy aspirations. Particularly, I thank my mother, who inspired me to be curious, passionate, and ambitious early on. When things feel impossible, she is the one who reminds me that every problem has a solution, it's just a matter of changing my mindset. I am grateful for my father, who not only spends countless hours driving me back and forth for research interviews and conferences but also makes time for daily discussions on current events, research, and whatnot (it's always a highlight of my day). I thank my younger sister Jessica for being my best friend–someone who can always put a smile on my face–and for reading an early version of this book to give effective feedback. And, to my grandparents, thank you for instilling the value and power of education deep into this family. They have been the ones who showed me how being a lifelong learner changes not only an individual's life, but the individual's family and future generations' lives.

Thirdly, I must give my special thanks to the team at Post Hill Press for helping to make this book happen. To my editors, Debra Englander, Caitlin Burdette, Ashlyn Inman, and HB Steadham, for believing in me and giving ever-insightful guidance, thoughtful editing, and enthusiasm for the book. And, to the designer of this book's beautiful cover Conroy Accord, thank you for your patience as I nitpicked with endless comments.

Fourthly, my sincere appreciation goes to Dr. Marlene Kanga, President of the World Federation of Engineering Organizations (2017-2019) and Vice President of the International Network for Women Engineers and Scientists (2011-2017) for being so kind to write a foreword for this book.

Finally, I have a wide range of experts, scholars, and stakeholders who have made the preparation of this book possible with their support, whether it was reviewing earlier drafts, offering encouragement and inspiration, or bringing diverse perspectives and disciplinary backgrounds to this book. In this context, I would like to sincerely thank them. They are mentioned alphabetically by name: Dr. Alfred Watkins (Founder and CEO of the Global Solutions Summit), Dr. Ameenah Gurib-Fakim (President of the Republic of Mauritius [2015-2018], biodiversity scientist), Ms. Amy Meuers (CEO of the National Youth Leadership Council [NYLC], USA), Ms. Anna Radulovski (Founder of the WomenTech Network), Mr. Anthony Le (Youth Engagement and Events Coordinator at NYLC, USA), Ms. Arlene Harris (Founder, Chairwoman at Wrethink, Inc.), Dr. Brian Baird (Chair and Founder at the National Museum and Center for Service, USA), Ms. Carolina Rojas Echeverri (Science Policy Interface Technology Focal Point at the United Nations Major Group for Children and Youth Youth), Ms. Dawn Cotter-Jenkins (Speaker Coach at TEDxDeerPark), Dr. Clapperton Chakanetsa Mavhunga (Professor of Science, Technology, and Society at the Massachusetts Institute of Technology [MIT]), Dr. E. William Colglazier (American physicist, the 4th Science and Technology Adviser to the U.S. Secretary of State), Dr. Emily Stewart (Senior Director of Education and Curation at Milton J. Rubenstein Museum of Science & Technology, New York), Dr. Giovanni Durante (Principal at Syosset High School, New York), Mr. Gregory Ryan (Retired Project Beyond Teacher at South Woods Middle School, New York), Ms. Gretchen Storer (Operations at Girls Leadership Academy Meetup [GLAM]), Dr. Huadong Guo (Director General of the International Research Center of Big Data for Sustainable Development Goals, Academician of the Chinese Academy of Sciences), Dr. Heide Hackmann (Director of Future Africa at the University of Pretoria, South Africa, and Inaugural CEO of the International Science Council), Ms. Inesa Vidas (Conference Project Manager for the Global Conference on Women's Studies), Ms. Jaclyn Stief (Director of Programming and Global Policy at BridgingTheGap Ventures), Dr. James R. Delisle (retired Professor of Education at Kent State University and author of The Gifted Teen Survival Guide), Dr. Janet Abbate (Professor, Science, Technology and Society at Virginia Tech), Dr. Jayshree Seth (3M Chief Science Advocate and Corporate Scientist), Dr. Jeffrey Sachs (University Professor and Director of the Center for Sustainable Development at Columbia University), Ms. Julie Rogers Bascom (Director of Learning & Leadership at NYLC), Mr. Kaleb Sy (Student at Columbia University, member of the NYLC Youth Advisory Council [2021-2023]), Dr. Linda A. Longmire (Professor of Global Studies and Geography, Women Studies Advisor and Director for Center for Civic Engagement at Hofstra University), Ms. Kaitlin Green (Program Manager at the New York Academy of Sciences), Ms. Margaret Sanchez (Director of Operations at GLAM), Dr. Michiharu Nakamura (President Emeritus, Japan Science and Technology Agency), Dr. Nathalie C. Lilavois (Curator and Executive Producer at TEDxDeerPark), Ms. Nuntiya Smith (Davidson Ambassador Program Manager at the Davidson Institute), Dr. Paulo Gadelha (President of FIOCRUZ [2009-2016], Coordinator of the FIOCRUZ Strategy for the 2030 Agenda), Dr. Quarraisha Abdool Karim (President of the World Academy of Sciences and UNAIDS Special Ambassador for Adolescents and HIV, Co-Founder and Scientific Director of the Centre for the AIDS Programme of Research in South Africa, Professor of Clinical Epidemiology at Columbia University), Dr. Richard Alexander Roehrl (Division for Sustainable Development Goals at the United Nations Headquarters, New York, USA), Mr. Richard Rusczyk (Founder and CEO of the Art of Problem Solving), Dr. Stuart Krusell (Senior Director, Global Programs, Sloan School of Management at MIT), Dr. Tom Rogers (Syosset

District Superintendent and CEO at Nassau BOCES, New York), Ms. Ursula Wynhoven (International Telecommunication Union [ITU] Representative to the United Nations, New York, Head of Its UN Affairs Division and NY Liaison Office, and Gender and Science Technology and Innovation Co-lead), Dr. Veerle Vandeweerd (Co-founder of the Global Sustainable Technology and Innovation Conference Series, Co-founder and Managing Partner Platform for Transformative Technologies, Principal Sustainability Officer/Member Advisory Board of Global Entrepreneurship Center, former Director of Environment and Energy at the United Nations Development Programme), Ms. Veronica Ade (Former Research Coordinator at Syosset High School, New York), Ms. Viola Zeqi Chen (Liaison Office to the United Nations at the ITU), and Dr. Xiaolan Fu (Professor of Technology and International Development, the Founding Director of the Technology and Management Centre for Development at the University of Oxford). I also want to extend my deep appreciation to the whole team at NYLC, the New York Academy of Sciences, the Davidson Institute, GLAM, Sharing to Empower, and the Scientific Committee of the Global Conference on Women's Studies for their support during my research journey.

All of these people made this book possible.

Lastly, I thank you, the reader, for taking the time to read this.

Credits have been given to Canva for allowing me to use their Free Content.

References

1000 Girls 1000 Futures. (2022). The New York Academy of Sciences. Date of access: 12/09/2022. https://www.nyas.org/programs/global-stem-alliance/1000-girls-1000-futures/

Abbas, F. A. et al. (2012). Why ethics in research are crucial? *Advances in Natural and Applied Sciences* 6(5):660-663.

American Psychological Association. (2023). Write with clarity, precision, and inclusion. Date of access: 1/25/2023. https://apastyle.apa.org/?_ga=2.227929429.950581259.1676823728-1793314810.1676823728

American Psychological Association. (2023). APA Style, Date of access: 1/25/2023. https://apastyle.apa.org/

Anderson, C. (2010). Presenting and evaluating qualitative research. *American Journal of Pharmaceutical Education* 74: 1–7.

Armstrong, N. (2023). Neil Armstrong quotes. Date of access: 1/25/2023. https://www.inspirationalstories.com/quotes/neil-armstrong-research-is-creating-new-knowledge/

Babbie, E. R. (2010). *The Practice of Social Research.* Belmont, CA: Wadsworth Cengage.

Babbie, E. R. (2020). Introduction: What is research? *The Basics of Social Research.* Belmont, CA: Wadsworth Cengage.

Bensimon, E. M. et al. (2004). Doing research that makes a difference. *The Journal of Higher Education,* 75(1):104–126.

Bhandari, P. (2020). An introduction to quantitative research. *Scribbr,* November 24. Date of access: 10/09/2022. https://www.scribbr.com/methodology/quantitative-research

Blaxter, L. et al. (2010). *How to Research,* New York: Open University Press.

Bouchrika, I. (2022). Top 10 qualities of good academic research. *Research.* Oct 11. Date of access: 10/20/2022. https://research.com/research/top-10-qualities-of-good-academic-research#2

Bradford, A. (2017). Empirical evidence: A definition. *Live Science,* July 28. Date of access: 10/20/2022. https://www.livescience.com/21456-empirical-evidence-a-definition.html

Brainy Quote. (2023). Date of access: 1/30/2023. https://www.brainyquote.com/quotes/marcus_aurelius_118558

Brown. B. (2023). Trust in emergence: Grounded theory and my Research Process. Date of access: 2/3/23. https://brenebrown.com/the-research/

Cambridge University Press. (2023). Areas of study. Date of access: 1/5/2023. https://www.cambridge.org/academic/author-services/areas-of-study/

Clear, J. (2018). *Atomic Habits*, New York: Avery.

Cotter, M. (2021). Margaret C. Anderson, Founder of *The Little Review*. Literary Ladies Guide. March 22. Date of access: October 28, 2022. https://www.literaryladiesguide.com/other-rad-voices/margaret-c-anderson-founder-of-the-little-review/

Denzin, N. K. and Lincoln, Y. S. (2005). Introduction: The discipline and practice of qualitative research. In *The Sage Handbook of Qualitative Research*, edited by Denzin N. K. and Lincoln, Y. S. Thousand Oaks, CA: Sage.

Denzin, N. K. and Lincoln, Y. S. (2005). *The Sage Handbook of Qualitative Research*, edited by Denzin, N. K. and Lincoln, Y. S. Thousand Oaks, CA: Sage.

Denzin, N. K. and Yvonna, S. L. (2005). *Handbook of Qualitative Research*. Sage: Thousand Oaks, CA: Sage.

Discover PhDs. (2020). What is research? – Purpose of research. Date of access: 9/21/2022. https://www.discoverphds.com/blog/what-is-research-purpose-of-research

Emerald Publishing. (2023). What are ethnographic methods? Date of access: 9/25/2022. https://www.emeraldgrouppublishing.com/how-to/observation/use-ethnographic-methods-participant-observation

Elsevier. (2022). How to write your references quickly and easily. Date of access: 9/20/2022. https://scientific-publishing.webshop.elsevier.com/manuscript-preparation/how-to-write-your-references-quickly-and-easily/

Elsevier. (2022). Literature review in research writing." Date of access: 9/20/2022. https://scientific-publishing.webshop. elsevier.com/research-process/importance-literature-review-research-writing/

Fisher, S. (2021). 17 research quotes to inspire and amuse you. February 4. Date of access: 10/20/2022. https://www.qualtrics. com/blog/research-quotes/

Gonçalves, C. D. S. and Liu, G. C. (2022). Space power: Utilizing satellites to bring electricity to the most vulnerable groups in Sub-Saharan Africa – Young innovators Camila dos Santos Gonçalves and Grace Chenxin Liu of the New York Academy of Sciences. The United Nations SDG Learn Podcast. Jun 23. https:// www.unsdglearn.org/podcast/space-power-utilizing-satel-lites-to-bring-electricity-to-the-most-vulnerable-groups/

Golesh, D., Baba Girei, Z., and Ibrahim, F. (2019). The role of logic in research. *International Journal of Scientific & Engineering Research, 10*(10), 894–904.

Goodman, J. et al. (2014). A few Goodmen: Surname-sharing economist coauthors. *Economic Inquiry.* Date of access: 8/20/2022. https://onlinelibrary.wiley.com/doi/abs/10.1111/ecin.12167

Good Reads. (2023). Quotes. Date of access: 12/28/2022. https:// www.goodreads.com/author/quotes

Hammersley, M., & Traianou, A. (2012). *Ethics in Qualitative Research: Controversies and Contexts.* London: Sage Publications.

Hutto, C. (2022). 32 powerful & empowering Michelle Obama quotes. Inhersight. June 23.

Israel, M. and Hay, I. (2006). *Research Ethics for Social Scientist,* SAGE Publications.

Jansen, D. and Warren K. (2020). What is research methodology? *GradCoach.* June 21. Date of access: 8/27/2022. https://gradcoach.com/what-is-research-methodology/

Jourdane, J. (2017) Fieldwork Fail: The Messy Side of Science, Makisapa. http://fieldworkfail.com/

Knuth, D. E. (1984). The toilet paper problem. *The American Mathematical Monthly.* Vol. 91, No. 8. 465–470.

List 25. (2022). 25 Extremely bizarre research papers. Date of access: 9/2/2022. https://list25.com/25-extremely-bizarre-research-papers/

Liu, G. C. (2022). Breaking the barriers in women's fencing: Historical roots, Title IX and empowerment of women. *Journal of International Women's Studies.* 24(3). July 17.

Liu, G. C. (2022). The gender digital divide: A review and future research agenda from a feminist perspective. Proceedings of the 4th Global Conference on Women's Studies. Nov 24, 2022.

Mavs Open Press. (2023). Disseminating your findings. University of Texas at Arlington Libraries. Date of access: 9/28/2022. https://uta.pressbooks.pub/foundationsofsocialworkresearch/chapter/12-2-disseminating-your-findings/

Merriam, S. B. (2009). *Qualitative Research: A Guide to Design and Implementation.* San Francisco, CA: Jossey-Bass.

McAdoo, M. (2015). *The Student's Survival Guide to Research.* Chicago: Neal-Schuman.

Muijs, D. (2010). *Doing Quantitative Research in Education with SPSS.* London: Sage.

Mandela, N. (2000). Speech by Nelson Mandela at the Inaugural Laureus Lifetime Achievement Award, Monaco 2000. Nelson Mandela Foundation. World Laureus Sports Awards Limited.

Office of Undergraduate Research. (2022). Why do research? The University of Montana. Date of access: 9/12/2022. https://www.umt.edu/ugresearch/research/why-research.php

O'Leary, Z. (2017). *The Essential Guide to Doing Your Research Project.* SAGE Publications.

Ollhoff, J. (2022). *How to Write a Literature Review,* Sparrow Media Group.

Pathak V. et al. (2013). Qualitative Research, *Perspectives in Clinical Research.* 4(3). July–Sep.

Patton, M. Q. (2002). *Qualitative research & evaluation methods.* Thousand Oaks, CA: Sage Publications.

Research Process. (2022). Literature review in research writing. Date of access: 9/12/2022. https://scientific-publishing.webshop.elsevier.com/research-process/importance-literature-review-research-writing/

Richard, A. K. and Casey, M. A. (2000). *Focus Groups. A Practical Guide for Applied Research.* Thousand Oaks, CA: Sage.

Science Buddies. (2022). How to format your research paper. Date of access: 11/12/2022. https://www.sciencebuddies.org/science-fair-projects/science-fair/how-to-format-a-research-paper

Sithole, S. (2016). Conducting research for the first time: Experiences of undergraduate social work students. *Southern African Journal of Social Work and Social Development.* 28(1):85, July.

Stahl, A. (2023). Will ChatGPT replace your job? *Forbes.* March 3. Date of access: 3/20/2023. https://www.forbes.com/sites/ashleystahl/2023/03/03/will-chatgpt-replace-your-job/?sh=72c999e51bed

Thattamparambil, N. (2020). How to choose the research methodology best suited for your study. *Editage Insights,* Feb 17. Date of access: 12/12/2022. https://www.editage.com/insights/how-to-choose-the-research-methodology-best-suited-for-your-study

The Concord Review. (2020). Submissions. Date of access: 12/29/2020. https://tcr.org/submit

The Junior Academy. (2023). The New York Academy of Sciences. Date of access: 12/12/2021. https://www.nyas.org/programs/global-stem-alliance/the-junior-academy/

The Office of Research Integrity. (2023). Module 1: Introduction: What is research? Date of access: 12/29/2022. https://ori.hhs.gov/module-1-introduction-what-research

The Society for Science. (2022). Ethics statement. Date of access: 11/19/2022. https://www.societyforscience.org/isef/international-rules/rules-for-all-projects/#Ethics

The University of Montana.(2022). Why do research? Date of access: 09/29/2022. https://www.umt.edu/ugresearch/research/why-research.php

The World Intellectual Property Organization. (2014). The human factor: The fundamental driver of innovation. Date of access: 1/25/2023. https://www.wipo.int/edocs/pubdocs/en/wipo_pub_gii_2014-intro2.pdf.

Tufte, E. R. (2001) *The Visual Display of Quantitative Information.* Cheshire, Connecticut: Graphics Press.

Turban, S. (2023). The complete guide to publishing your research in high school. Date of access: 12/27/2022. https://www.lumiere-education.com/post/the-complete-guide-to-publishing-your-research-in-high-school

U.S. Department of Education. (2022). Protection of human subjects in research, Date of access: 12/17/2020. https://www2.ed.gov/about/offices/list/ocfo/humansub.html

Virtues for Life. (2023). 10 inspiring quotes by Eleanor Roosevelt. Date of access: 11/28/2022. https://www.virtuesforlife.com/10-inspiring-quotes-by-eleanor-roosevelt/

Walden University. (2010). 7 research challenges (and how to overcome them). Date of access: 11/25/2020. https://www.waldenu.edu/news-and-events/publications/articles/2010/01-research-challenges

Wilson, et al. (2010). Disseminating research findings: what should researchers do? A systematic scoping review of conceptual framework. Implementation Science. 5(91).

Zongker, D. (2002). Chicken Chicken Chicken: Chicken Chicken. Date of access: October 28, 2022. https://isotropic.org/papers/chicken.pdf

Glossary

Animal care: The treatment of nonhuman animals used in research and experimentation. Various regulations, standards, and principles have been developed to protect the well-being of such animals and ensure that they are treated in a humane and ethical manner.

Archeologist: A person who studies human history and prehistory through the excavation of sites and the analysis of artifacts and other physical remains.

Avid: Having or showing a keen interest in or enthusiasm for something.

Biologist: An expert in or student of the branch of science concerning living organisms.

Confidentiality: An agreement that is formed between the researcher and participant, via the informed consent process, that ensures the participant's identity, personal information, responses, etc. will not be disclosed to anyone outside of the research team unless otherwise agreed upon.

Copyright: The exclusive legal right, given to an originator or an assignee to print, publish, perform, film, or record literary, artistic, or musical material, and to authorize others to do the same.

Criteria: A principle or standard by which something may be judged or decided.

Descriptive research: Focusing on expanding knowledge of current issues through data collection. It describes the behavior of a sample population.

Entomologist: A person who studies or is an expert in the branch of zoology concerned with insects.

Explanatory research: Understanding the impact of specific changes in existing standard procedures. This usually involves running experiments.

Exploratory research: Investigating a group of questions, especially new problem areas that haven't been explored before.

Fraud: Wrongful or criminal deception intended to result in financial or personal gain.

Human participant: According to Code of Federal Regulation 45, CFR 46, a human participant is a living individual about whom an investigator conducting research obtains (1) data or samples through intervention or interaction with individuals(s) or (2) identifiable private information.

Human participant protection: Laws set by the U.S. Department of Health and Human Services (DHHS) to protect a person from risks in research studies that any federal agency or department has a part in. Also called 45 CFR 46, 45 Code of Federal Regulations Part 46, and Protection of Human Subjects.

Human research: Any systematic investigation, including research development, testing, and evaluation, utilizing human subjects, that is designed to develop or contribute to generalized knowledge.

Index: An alphabetical list of names, subjects, etc., with references to the places where they occur, typically found at the end of a book.

Integrity: The quality of being honest and having strong moral principles.

Intellectual Property: A work or invention that is the result of creativity, such as a manuscript or a design, to which one has rights and for which one may apply for a patent, copyright, trademark, etc.

Invasive species: An introduced, nonnative organism (disease, parasite, plant, or animal) that begins to spread or expand its range from the site of its original introduction and that has the potential to cause harm to the environment, the economy, or to human health.

Jargon: Special words or expressions that are used by a particular profession or group and are difficult for others to understand.

Oncologist: A medical practitioner qualified to diagnose and treat tumors.

Organism: An individual animal, plant, or single-celled life form.

Patent: A government authority or license conferring a right or title for a set period, especially the sole right to exclude others from making, using, or selling an invention.

Pathogen: A bacterium, virus, or other microorganism that can cause disease.

Polymath: A person of wide-ranging knowledge or learning.

Potentially hazardous biological material: General term used to describe recombinant and synthetic nucleic acids, toxins, human, animal and plant pathogens requiring BSL-2 and higher and Select Agents that could cause disease in humans.

Practitioner: A person actively engaged in an art, discipline, or profession, especially medicine.

Prerequisite: A thing that is required as a prior condition for something else to happen or exist.

Rationale: A set of reasons or a logical basis for a course of action or a particular belief.

Reciprocity: The practice of exchanging things with others for mutual benefit, especially privileges granted by one country or organization to another.

Research integrity: The use of honest and verifiable methods in proposing, performing, and evaluating research. reporting research results with particular attention to adherence to rules, regulations, guidelines, and. following commonly accepted professional codes or norms.

Research mentor: A senior researcher, professor, teacher, or scholar who serves as a role model and coach to an individual student or junior researcher, or scholar in a formal relationship.

Research methods: The strategies, processes, or techniques utilized in the collection of data or evidence for analysis in order to uncover new information or create a better understanding of a topic. There are different types of research methods that use different tools for data collection.

Social media: Websites and applications that enable users to create and share content or to participate in social networking.

The United Nations Sustainable Development Goals (SDG): A collection of 17 interlinked objectives designed to serve as a "shared blueprint for peace and prosperity for people and the planet now and into the future". They are a call for action by all countries—poor, rich and middle-income—to promote prosperity while protecting the planet.

Volcanologist: A volcanologist, or volcano scientist, is a geologist who focuses on understanding the formation and eruptive activity of volcanoes.

Scrutinize: Examine or inspect closely and thoroughly.

STATA: A general-purpose statistical software package developed by StataCorp for data manipulation, visualization, statistics, and automated reporting.

Systematic: Done or acting according to a fixed plan or system; methodical.

R: A programming language for statistical computing and graphics supported by the R Core Team and the R Foundation for Statistical Computing.

Python: A high-level, general-purpose programming language.

Tableau: A visual analytics platform transforming the way we use data to solve problems—empowering people and organizations to make the most of their data. Tableau helps people see and understand data.

Validate: Check or prove the validity or accuracy of (something).

About the Author

GRACE CHENXIN LIU IS RECOGNIZED globally as a youth researcher, advocate, and change-maker for gender equality and sustainable development. She successfully worked on fourteen projects and had multiple peer-reviewed journal publications before she turned fifteen. She has inspired students across six continents and from over 140 countries as the highlighted speaker at many organizations including the United Nations SDG Learncast, the International Telecommunication Union, the Society of Women Engineers, TEDx, Girls Leadership Academy Meetup, and more.

Grace is a 2023 World Science Scholar, WomenTech Global Rising Star of the Year Award winner, a Global Youth Challenge winner, and a member of the winning team of the global Fall 2022 Junior Academy Challenge. She is a 2022–2024 Youth Advisory Council member of the National Youth Leadership Council, part of the Davidson Institute's Ambassador Program's Class of 2024, the youngest member of the Global Conference on Women's Studies Scientific Committee, and a 2022 Equality & Inclusion Working Group Leader at YOUNGA by BridgingTheGap Ventures.

Grace founded Research to Empower, an educational non-profit working to inspire, support, and empower the next generation of aspiring young researchers. Its mission is to make research accessible and fun to all, regardless of age, gender, race, or financial background. She is also the founder of Sharing to Empower, an international alliance researching and promoting gender equality and sustainable development with global impact and local reach.